"A luminous journey from worry to its surp.... delight. A book laden with richness, humor, honesty, and hope. We *can* worry less and live more. Both practical and delightful. Start reading. Stop worrying. Start living."

—Anita Lustrea, co-host of *Midday Connection*,
speaker, author of *What Women Tell Me*

"Jane Rubietta's new book inspires me to make snow angels in the snow, plant flowers in the spring, ride my bike in the summer, and slow down long enough to deeply appreciate the colors of fall. Most of us move too fast, worry too often, and miss much of what God wants to show us about himself and his creation. Jane's book is a poetic, beautiful reminder that more rests on God's shoulders than on mine, and it pleases him when I nurture a heart at rest so I can actually live by faith. I wholeheartedly endorse this book."

—Susie Larson, national radio host
and speaker, and author
of *Your Beautiful Purpose*

"The problem with worry is that our minds and bodies conspire to keep us unaware. Jane's words are a powerful antidote to that. Considering delight, memory, dreams, movement, spontaneity, and more, she weaves a journey against the worry that separates us from ourselves and from the good God who made us."

—Nancy Ortberg, author of *Looking for God:
An Unexpected Journey Through Tattoos,
Tofu, and Pronouns*

"With piercing honesty and gentle humor, Jane Rubietta takes aim at one of the biggest enemies of our joy—worry. She then provides an arsenal of practical tools to destroy this enemy. And she does it with flowing prose and healing words. This book had me laughing and weeping, and eager to try her creative ideas so I can begin to worry less and live more."

—Lynn Austin, Christy Award–winning author

"God wants us to live more and worry less, but worry is stealing the pleasure from our lives. Jane Rubietta has masterfully written a book that is a soothing balm to the worry-worn soul. She will take you on an exciting discovery of the delight of God—the secret to defeating worry—enabling you to embrace the worry-free life again.

—Shelly Esser, editor, *Just Between Us*

"Vintage Jane! Telling stories. Being real. Giving practical biblical wisdom—about the worry that stalks us all. If you want handholds to grab as you scale your own walls of anxiety, let Jane hand you her own tools. Tools of play, self-nurture, memory, spontaneity, trust, and more."

—Adele Ahlberg Calhoun, co–lead pastor
at Redeemer Community Church,
spiritual director, and author

"Join the healing journey to slow down, savor, and thrive in wholeness. Jane is our expert guide providing practical tools for the worry-wrinkled soul toward breakthrough, healing, and encountering God's love and delight."

—Dr. Catherine Hart Weber, therapist and author,
Flourish: Discover Vibrant Living

"Who doesn't want to *Worry Less So You Can Live More*? Jane Rubietta masterfully provides amazing, insightful 'Tools' wrapped in stories from the heart of a worrier, taking the reader from being weighed down with worry to the realization that 'living more' is just around the corner when we intentionally and consistently reposition our souls to focus and delight in Jesus! Challenging and inspiring read!"

—Edna Mapstone, national director,
Great Commission Women of the Christian
and Missionary Alliance

Worry Less
So You Can
Live More

Worry Less
So You Can
Live More

SURPRISING, SIMPLE WAYS
TO FEEL MORE PEACE,
JOY, AND ENERGY

Jane Rubietta

BETHANY HOUSE PUBLISHERS

a division of Baker Publishing Group
Minneapolis, Minnesota

Published by Bethany House Publishers
11400 Hampshire Avenue South
Bloomington, Minnesota 55438
www.bethanyhouse.com

Bethany House Publishers is a division of
Baker Publishing Group, Grand Rapids, Michigan

Printed in the United States of America

Library of Congress Cataloging-in-Publication Data
Rubietta, Jane.
    Worry less so you can live more : surprising, simple ways to feel more peace, joy, and energy / Jane Rubietta.
      pages cm
    Includes bibliographical references.
    Summary: "Invites women to leave behind anxiety and worry to experience life, delight, and rest in God, who cares for them moment by moment. Includes discussion questions and journaling prompts"— Provided by publisher.
    ISBN 978-0-7642-1265-9 (pbk. : alk. paper)
    1. Christian women—Religious life. 2. Worry—Religious aspects—Christianity. 3. Anxiety—Religious aspects—Christianity. I. Title.
    BV4527.R826 2015
    248.8′43—dc23
                                     2014041494

In keeping with biblical principles of creation stewardship, Baker Publishing Group advocates the responsible use of our natural resources. As a member of the Green Press Initiative, our company uses recycled paper when possible. The text paper of this book is composed in part of post-consumer waste.

Cover design by Greg Jackson, Thinkpen Design, Inc.

15 16 17 18 19 20 21   7 6 5 4 3 2 1

For Bonnie,
Who shared her flowers
And listened
Always directing my heart
To God

I want to thank all the people over the years
who have shared my life
and shared their stories with me:
your fears, your laughter, your hope, and your faith.
Thank you for being those
who continue to trust your lives
to the God who is unseen.

Contents

Reader Beware

These are at times whimsical but thoughtful musings of a journey toward wholeness, toward worrying less and living more. They are not a doctrinal dissertation, nor a theological tome. If you feel you have Generalized Anxiety Disorder, suffer from panic attacks, or deal with other serious problems, then please seek professional help, and take this book with you.

Worry Less So You Can Live More is not intended to solve the problems of the world or represent an argument for any particular camp; it is not an exegesis of a particular book in the Bible. I don't think we need more knowledge, necessarily, although that is not a bad thing. But knowledge cannot substitute for the brilliance of being loved by God.

This journey has dragged me through thistle and briar patch, and along the way I have found that women everywhere struggle with similar issues: of trust, of exhaustion, of longing, always with both the overarching minor descant and bass line of worry. We mostly feel a little bit lost in the heaviness of the struggle. It is a pleasure to know that en route, our wildflower-throwing God waits with delight to surprise us and love us.

So please don't send me angry letters arguing about my priorities in a world that is dying. I'm afraid that we are dying, as well. If we are dead, we are useless to this world. And God calls us to do more than just stay alive until Jesus returns for us. God wants us to live more, and worry less, and along the way, to live in his delight.

Worry Less So You Can Live More is my attempt to relinquish my worry-wrinkled soul, to encounter the delight of God and the God of delight, and to share my findings with others.

Introduction

The lightning bugs called our names in the dusk, their mysterious invitational glow rising up from the dewy grass of early summer. Fun jammed most every day. We made mud pies, laughed until our sides hurt, lay down in the field behind my house, and created catapults from the tall weeds with their little bullet-shaped seed heads.

Long before the classic Indiana-based cycling movie *Breaking Away* hit our VCRs (actually before VCRs were perhaps even invented), we pedaled our bikes with a ferocity that could overtake the greatest Olympian, up and down the rolling hills of southern Indiana. On boiling hot days, we ran down the rocky driveway barefoot, squatted over the hot pavement, and popped tar bubbles with sticks and pointy stones. We swallowed peanut butter sandwiches or grilled cheeses and the requisite carrot sticks with our legs jiggling and feet tapping to get back outside. Hours later we rushed back inside for dinner, skidding into our seats at the table after a fast hands-and-face washing and pulling a comb through play-tangled mops of hair. Afterward, we each raced back outside and reassembled as though called by an inaudible whistle. When dusk approached, we stacked cans to kick, and chased each other playing Ghost in the Graveyard. We hunted fireflies with our jelly jars, diamond-shaped holes punched in the lids by my dad with a nail and hammer.

But when evening replaced the dusk and the streetlights pierced the darkness, our curtain fell. Jars teeming with lightning bugs, we headed for home. Dirt and sweat coated our skin, and satisfaction filled our hearts. A quick bath, a cool clean bed, a good-night kiss. A perfect summer day.

We raced from delight to delight, and never recognized the gift. We were children. Our work was to play.

All Work and No Play . . .

Last year, I read the pronouncement of the angel Gabriel to John the Baptist's father: "You will have great joy and gladness . . ." (Luke 1:14 NLT).[1] I burst into tears in the quiet dawn. Where was that promise being fulfilled in my life? Work occupies my waking hours, and if I'm not working, I'm worrying about work. But I *do* work; I almost never *don't* work. I work three jobs, between my spiritual calling, my office (the necessary foundation undergirding that calling), and my family. I have become a zombie of sorts, with the lifeblood of joy and gladness sucked from my veins.

Like so many people, I work seven days a week, week after week. I work from my house most weekdays, so home is not a sanctuary set apart from work. No longer do I fall into bed with a jar full of fireflies illuminating my face, or friends' voices singing through my memory along with the exhilaration of the wind on my face as I raced down hills. I just fall into bed. Exhausted. The sheets aren't even cool in the muggy Chicago nights, nor are they necessarily clean, because no one else changes them. Except for the sweat from living and working in a home without air-conditioning, there's no grime from my day to shower off, no bug spray left over from eager play, because I am either desk-bound or airport-bound.

Looking at my life now, I wonder: Where did that little girl go? Has she played hide-and-seek, waiting for me to find her? Has she been in her hiding spot for so long that she blends in with the rocks and trees? Has she petrified, become a statue like one of the woodland creatures in *The Chronicles of Narnia*, where it is always winter, never summer? The adage is true, though it doesn't seem economically feasible to reverse: All work and no play makes Jane a dull girl. Add on what is practically an IV line of worry, and I am beyond dull. I am comatose of heart.

A few weeks after my dawn-burst of tears over the sad state of my soul, my husband returned from a ministerial meeting (yawn) and stuck a penciled sticky note on my chest. He poked his finger onto the paper for emphasis. "Call her. You need to call this woman."

The woman lived nearby, and Rich thought she would be a good friend to walk with me toward the forgotten fields of childhood. I wore the note for the rest of the day, debating, and the next morning grabbed the phone from its cradle. It was time, past time, to pay attention to this little girl. It was time to re-parent that lost child who loved to play but got forgotten in the overdrive of my life. To discover her again, listen to her child-heart, beckon her out of hiding.

The sticky-note lady invited me over and was as warm in person as a summer day at the beach. She turned out to be one of those rare people who live in God's delight consistently, and when we get together, my soul feels tended and attended. The tables turn during those occasional minutes. Rather than my asking the questions and inviting people deeper, she asks me deep, thoughtful questions. These intervening months are teaching me to listen to, and honor, my own heart. And God's heart.

The result? A journey—sometimes exhilarating, like riding a bike down winding southern hills; sometimes exhausting, like tromping up the hill with a flat tire—toward reversing worry and recapturing delight.

The Wrinkled-Brow Disease

Worry. Isn't worry the disease behind our work-all-day lives? And it's stealing our lives.

Each weekend, at conferences and retreats, I see women weighed down by worry. Heavyhearted at the state of their marriages, or their children, or both, or lack of either. Disappointed because of the sheer drudgery of the day-after-day trudge through life. Where have our hopes disappeared? Whatever happened to the joy of our salvation? It has vanished in our drooping economy, our drowsy spirits, our often-dreary churches (hey, it's true).

Women worry. To compound their worries, they're sad, lonely, discouraged, scared, anxious, hurt, and exhausted. And they long for relief, the kind a cranky child experiences after sitting on a parent's lap, being held and loved, then jumping down and running off carefree, knowing "it's all being taken care of." Even better, "*I'm being taken care of.*" *Worry Less So You Can Live More* offers the antithesis of worry, an invitation from Jesus himself, who pats his lap, holds out beckoning hands, and says, "*Shhh. Shhh. Come. Sit. Look at me, looking at you, loving you.*"

Worry Less So You Can Live More encapsulates the longing to live worry-free, in childlike delight and freedom, without the stilted, tepid, or frightening phrases of traditional Christianity. For example, the overused, little understood word *joy* that brings visions of children marching in place during Sunday school, looking serious and ready to battle the conquistadors, spouting the acronym J=Jesus (first), O=others (second), Y=you (last). It can be misleading, a recipe for depression. Spirituality with Christ at the core should not be depressing.

I hate to state the obvious, but really? One glance at my face on any given day, and no one would *want* my Jesus. Worry lines ride between my eyebrows like a railroad track.

But that doesn't have to be the end of the story. Because there's an antidote for the disease of worry: delight. We can replace worry with delight, exchange deadly worry for real life. Isn't it time, past time? Time to learn to live again, to live in the moment-by-moment pleasure of a God who has the whole world in his hand, a God who smiles at our antics, delights in our childlike hearts, and wants us to trust him enough to learn to rest and play and enjoy him again. To delight in the God who delights in us. The One who promised us life can help us forego worry and live in delight.

Using This Resource

Because we are quantifiers, people who want 1-2-3 steps to success, because we want to see tools that will help us take those steps, this book is designed for maximum practicality and application. I'm not a doctor, an analyst, a psychiatrist, or a researcher. I'm writing about worry because I'm an expert . . . in worrying. And I figure, since Nietzsche said, "Whatever doesn't kill you makes you stronger," maybe I'm strong enough to take notes along the way, to share what is working for me. And plus, I'm not dead, so worrying hasn't killed me.

But because I'm a quantifier and a skeptic and a tightwad, I want stuff that actually works—whether it's the lemon squeezer in my kitchen (it works great!) or the free curbside lawn mower (it works, sometimes), or Christianity. Especially I want to know that Jesus makes a difference and that all the words in the Bible really do work . . . if you work them, as they say in twelve-step programs. Still, I don't have a lot of patience with cookbook-style, formulaic faith. *Worry Less So You Can Live More* is not a checklist, so that at the end you can say, "I've done this, and this, and this . . ." Faith is a step-by-step choice that we make every single day of our lives, and that's the only way to work with worry. Step after step after stumble after struggle after . . . step.

Perhaps you will want to start a special journal where you process your *Worry Less So You Can Live More* progress so you have some proof of your travels, your movement away from worry toward delight. The application section of each chapter contains a quote from a contemporary or classic author, and a Scripture passage for meditation. There are questions that a spiritual friend or mentor might ask, designed to foster deeper understanding of our souls and thus kindness toward ourselves, as well as actual change in our worrisome lives. These lead into a prayer, called *Votum*, meaning prayer, offering, wish, or desire. This *Votum* we might offer to God is another means of jump-starting our relationship with God and of being honest with ourselves about our battle with worry. *Benedictus*, typically a prayer sung at the end of worship, is a "saying well" message that God might sing over us, answering our anxious or heartfelt prayer.

Take time with the application section. Slow down enough to savor the quote. Ask yourself, "How does this fit with the chapter subject? How does this sync with my life? Or does it? Do I want it to?" Read the Scriptures meditatively. Read them aloud. Repeat them until they begin to sink into your soul. Maybe you want to memorize the Scriptures so you have immediate retrieval of God's Word. Write them on a 3 x 5 card and carry them with you throughout your day, your week. Try the tool of *lectio divina*, or sacred reading, that involves reading the passage and then listening, waiting, hearing your own soul reaction, and inviting God to show you how to apply the Word, what it means to you and for you. Read the Scripture again and repeat the listening, waiting, hearing, and inviting several times, slowly.

Try reading both the *Votum* and the *Benedictus* aloud, so you have both the audio and visual senses involved. Always, in all of these tools, listen for your soul's response and respect your inner self enough to wait, and listen, and take the time necessary for breakthrough and for healing. You are worth it, your soul is worth it, and your heart is worth it. You are not alone. We all need to begin to heal from our worrisome lives.

Journey Toward Delight

When we were children playing Kick the Can, fighting the mosquitoes, and smelling like bug repellent (thanks, Mr. Deet), the person who was *it* would shout, "Come out, come out, wherever you are!" And we all came running, trying to be the first to kick the can or set the prisoners free without being caught.

This journey toward delight as an adult has sometimes been more "mosquito bites" than "lightning bugs." It's encompassed fear, poor communication, codependence, grief, unforgiveness, and the common denominator for all these issues: worry. I've uncovered painful memories and revisited some serious character defects. But, unlike scratching those bites with their endless itching and keeping them raw, these discoveries are leading me toward healing. It has been a surprise, to be honest. A little like running to kick the can and actually setting the prisoners free.

There are fireflies en route, as well, as I've met up again with the God who throws garlands of hosannas around my neck, who rips off my mourning band and tosses a lei of wildflowers over my head. As we journey together, I am moving, as the psalmist says, from wild lament to whirling dance (Psalm 30:11).

And today, with the rain tumbling against the roof overhead, I hear again the invitation, and call it out for that lost (and getting found) little girl who loved (*loves*) to play: "Come out, come out, wherever you are!" Or even, "Rain, rain, go away, my friends and I want to play."

So off we go. Join me on this journey away from worry and toward simple delight, as we listen a little more to our hearts, and move a little more toward unexpected life. Toward connecting with the God who delights in us. The God of yesterday can take care of tomorrow's worries and help us live in today.

We can learn to worry less and live more. Delight *is* possible. I have the petals for proof.

1

Wearing Wildflowers
The Tool of Play

*Beginning to heal from a work-and-worry-all-day
mentality to a wildflowers-on-the-way lifestyle.*

She rushed out the back door on toddler legs, with a smile
the color of morning bursting over her face. Her blond hair
shone in the southern Indiana sun as she bobbed and laughed
and reached out little hands to the tulips.

At almost four, our daughter Ruthie's task was to gather flowers
for her auntie's bridal shower, and gather them she did. Fist after
fist of long-stemmed beauties, a rainbow of blooms. These giants
were half her height, but even their color-wheel vibrancy was no
match for her innocence, her sunny brilliance and delight.

To her alive little heart, the tulips were wild, and they were put
on earth for her to pick. My parents' backyard generously offered
up these blooms from borders of perennials interspersed with all
sorts of weeds.

And my parents loved watching Ruthie love those flowers. She danced through the yard, her curls bouncing, the blooms waving and bowing like dancers themselves.

Even now, twenty-some years later, I remember and smile. And I think God, who lives outside of time, smiles, too. Loving this little girl, loving her eager embrace of the beauty he provided, loving her wildflower dance.

How does that dance disappear as we grow older? I don't remember when I stopped dancing. I don't remember if I ever danced, aside from the fist-waving '70s and '80s gyrations we loosely (or optimistically) called dancing. But I do remember that graduating from college was a clanging alarm to awaken and arise to somber adulthood responsibilities. In seminary, after discovering William Law's little book *A Serious Call to a Devout and Holy Life* (1728), I thought, *This is true. It's serious business, being a Christian.* And we have the hymns to prove it: "Onward, Christian Soldiers," "We'll Work 'Til Jesus Comes."

I quit reading fiction—too frivolous if people are perishing. No more cracking jokes. Somewhere along the journey I stopped laughing, lost all perspective and balance. Everything seemed overly important, everything an issue, whether it was paying two cents too much for a gallon of milk or gasoline (Good Christian Women save money, and furrow our brows while doing so) or being two minutes late for a commitment.

But all this seriousness is killing me. It's killing my heart, probably literally, but also figuratively. *Joie de vivre*—joy of living, of life—is not a reality, only a fun French phrase. Isn't the root of such dreadful seriousness . . . worry? And isn't worry a misunderstanding of the God who carries the whole world in his hands? We move from that childlike, tulip-picking innocence, from living without a worry in the world, to worrying and carrying the weight of the world on our shoulders—and our soul.

This all became clear to me one day with my sticky-note friend, who loved me enough to ask me about my workload. She'd had no idea how many hours I work, how intense the desktop portion of that work, or how much I loathe all the administration—that it can eat up my entire creative life, that it forces me into my left-brain, fear-filled, there's-not-enough-to-go-around hemisphere.

Rather than the pseudo, Sunday-only smile that vanishes into a teeth-gritting grimace the rest of the week, this friend's face displays the quiet radiance of a road-tested woman who's found God's love beyond adequate in her life. She talks about nothing she doesn't know through living it. In fact, she is the face of delight for me. She lives in a profound attentiveness to God's presence—which may be the secret to delight, to anti-worry living—noticing and connecting with God, who finds delight everywhere. So when she speaks, I listen.

"Jane, you need help in your office."

Uh, duh, I thought, then nodded and protested aloud from the shadow-side of my soul, "I can't afford help." I heaved a mountainous sigh. "And no one wants to volunteer."

"Why would they want to volunteer?"

Well. Right. Good question. Just the journey to my desk requires ample liability and health insurance coverage because of the important and not-too-important litter en route. (Note to self: Investigate workman's comp. Or in this case, workwoman's.) Besides, they couldn't find the desk. But if they could locate the wooden structure beneath the piles of papers and books, they would be befuddled before they began. We could run a special edition of *Survivor* for people who venture into my office.

Her question silenced us both, except that my little child-heart started wringing its hands and running around like a mouse in a cage parked over open flames.

One thing about my friend is that she waits for me, waits for my brain to stop panicking and to shake out the words that describe my soul's state. "My needs hit me at my desk, especially when I return from a trip." I brought this out with hesitation, feeling my way, though it was far from profound. "I need to do bookwork.

I need to answer seven hundred emails. I need to send speaking contracts, or PR, or make phone calls to church leaders . . ."

More silence. A gentle nod of her head.

Finally, she asked, "Jane, do you think God wants to meet your needs?"

I raised my eyebrows and started to nod, then stopped. Obviously, the right answer, the I-grew-up-in-Sunday-school answer, is *yes*. "I think it's pretty scriptural," I finally said. I'm not sure if I was being wry or sarcastic, or self-deprecating, or probably all three. "You know Philippians 4:19: 'My God will meet all your needs according to the riches of his glory in Christ Jesus.'"

Then I stopped again. I am slow to connect the dots on the map when riding the rails of the worry train. How had I missed this? *All my needs.* The Sunday-school side of my brain believes this, but the faith side? *All my needs?* Wouldn't that be something?

"If God is present to you during your time in Scripture and prayer, why can't God also be present to you at your desk?"

Silence again. My soul stopped its mouse-running, and wringing, and listened.

Invite God to work with me at my desk, to share that dreaded, overwhelming, worrisome task? To treat God like a *companion* helping me? Seriously? That sounds like a worry remedy to me.

I hauled in a lungful of air. Someone had just loosened my straitjacket.

All my needs. This rolled around in my soul like a marble in an empty moving van. Paul doesn't say, "God will meet some, a few, the bare minimum of your needs." Or, only the needs on the bottom level of Abraham Maslow's pyramid, like air, water, food, and sleep—so far God's providing for those needs just fine. In fact, in this verse in Philippians, God doesn't define needs at all. *Humph.*

So what is the catch here? I tried to find some reason that this can't be true, a loophole. Just because it seems unbelievable to me—why would the God of the universe want to work alongside me, like some hired hand, or a volunteer?—doesn't mean it isn't true.

Part of my problem is paying attention. As soon as I leave my morning time with God, I develop some sort of amnesia. My worries pile up like rubble while I forge ahead into my dreadful desk tasks as though they are separate from my soul, and from my Savior. As though what happens ten feet away from my soul-breakfast with Jesus doesn't concern him at all. That's not true, for my brain and the Bible tell me so, but this spiritual ADHD kicks into gear. Or maybe I'm like a baby who plays with a rattle one minute, then drops it over the side of her high chair and instantly forgets about it. Pre-object permanence, only in this case it's pre-relationship permanence. I forget that I am always intricately tied to Jesus.

Or maybe it's that I move out of the relational side of my brain and into the "Onward, Christian Soldiers" side, and figure I just have to gut it out until I pack for my next flight or create space to write the next words for a book or article. Or until Jesus comes back and takes me to heaven.

But if Jesus never leaves us or forsakes us, then what about that desk time? Today, I balked at sitting in the office rubble until I became still. The morning had gotten away from me like a wild horse refusing to be corralled and broken. There was a storm in the night, sleep was fitful; my son needed breakfast and a gigantic packed lunch for a long day of physical workout, and then needed a ride to the train; my husband needed sandwiches for his commute. Before I knew it, 9:30 rolled by, and God couldn't slip a bite-sized word edgewise into the jaw of my tightly clenched morning.

So I sat. Outside, the newly cut grass looked like the Emerald City artist had slathered paint over it, the birds hopped about the lawn like kids on a scavenger hunt. I sat, opened the Scriptures, hovered over Psalm 33. I didn't try to learn the words in the original language, didn't compare other versions of Scripture. I didn't try to exegete or outline the chapter, or take notes for a speech or writing project.

> Watch this: God's eye is on those who respect him,
> the ones who are looking for his love.
> He's ready to come to their rescue in bad times;
> in lean times he keeps body and soul together.
> We're depending on God, he's everything we need.
> What's more, our hearts brim with joy
> Since we've taken for our own his holy name.
> Love us, God, with all you've got—
> That's what we're depending on.
>
> vv. 18–22 THE MESSAGE

I "watched this." I sat. I breathed. I directed my heart, without words, to God. I prayed with words, too, for the people I love and other concerns. I "watched this" some more, drinking in the beauty through the windows. The smudged and cobwebby windows.

When I climbed over the obstacles to my desk, an email confirmed an invitation to speak in Ohio next spring. And a pastor left a message about booking dates for a women's retreat.

When Ruthie still inhabited my womb, sometimes it felt like a prenatal gymnasium in there with her exercise routine. Now, thinking about those emails, I had a similar sensation in my soul—might God be meeting some of my needs? (A rhetorical question. Don't worry, I'm not entirely dense.) My heart turned a little somersault. My sticky-note friend says it's the work of the Holy Spirit, that flip-flopping.

Or else, it's the little flower-picking child appearing at last, showing her ecstatic response in the only way she knows how.

So this Philippians 4:19 promise seems to hold. But context is everything, for us as human beings and for this passage of Scripture.

Though I might doubt, Paul gets it. Life is a walk through barricades and land mines sometimes—maybe often, maybe most days. Paul had been shipwrecked and beaten almost to the last breath in his body, arrested, slammed in prison, and tortured. Earlier in Philippians 4, he says that he'd been starved; he'd eaten like a king. He says he learned to be content, to be at peace, in all those situations, not because he was superhuman or super-spiritual or exercised the power of positive thinking (which his words in verse 8 might suggest). But because of God's provision, because whether behind bars or hanging on to a plank in the midst of tossing seas, this Christ-follower found God to be faithful to his promises. So Paul could wrap up that entire, almost pious-sounding section with "My God will meet all your needs according to the riches of his glory in Christ Jesus."

If God could do it for Paul, could God—would God?—continue to do it for me, even though I'm not waging life-or-death battles like the apostle did? I don't have Paul's résumé. Could God supply my needs, not just this second at my desk, in this single incident, but day after day, year after year?

In research, the findings must be replicated by other studies before validation. So I resolve to watch and see.

When my kids were in school, our public schools sponsored career days for the students. But rather than inviting adults with various jobs to present speeches to the students, the schools offered "Take Your Child to Work Day." Rich and I were pretty sure that our children would not be enthralled with the possibility of going to work with us, since we primarily work out of our home during the week, unless it meant that they could sleep all day. Instead, my husband went after the spirit of the law, which was to interest students in various fields. Rich devised work visits with people whose careers paralleled our children's interests and gifts.

One year, he took our son Zak to a friend's studio in Chicago, where they record and layer in sound for high-profile commercials. With the Super Bowl looming, the day's audio projects included an ad for a popular sports drink. Our friend reworked the commercial using Zak's voice instead of the original broadcaster's, then gave Zak an audio recording of the tracks. His teacher played the tape the next day, and Zak's friends treated him like a celebrity.

On the momentous "Take Your Child to Work Day," the worst possible fate was being stuck at school in study hall with a few other lame students whose parents (also) had lame jobs. Our daughter and her friend were so eager to avoid that social disaster that they agreed to work for me. Ordering pizza for lunch helped. In the Land of Overwhelm at the home office, I welcomed their presence and created a list of research tasks for them. I still have 3 x 5 cards with their results, penned in round middle-school handwriting. It was my first experience having office help, and humbling that they worked without complaining at such basic jobs, freeing me for other tasks.

"Take Your Child to Work Days" were good days. For Rich, for me, and for our kids, for various reasons (getting out of school perhaps the primary benefit in their eyes). Why is it so hard for me to believe that Jesus would be really happy to come to work with me? To guide me in my office? I *know* he fills and inspires me, communicating through me when I'm speaking. And hopefully when I'm writing. Do I think desk work is beneath Jesus? (Of course, he's never seen my desk. Wait. That's not true.)

If Jesus is working alongside me, doesn't that render worry useless?

For my daily breakfast with God, I'm crawling my way through the Scriptures on about a five-year plan, and for this journey through, using *The Message* paraphrase of the Bible. David's words in Psalm 30:11–12 caught my heart and my fancy:

You did it: you changed wild lament
    into whirling dance;
You ripped off my black mourning band
    and decked me with wildflowers.
I'm about to burst with song;
    I can't keep quiet about you.
God, my God,
    I can't thank you enough.

THE MESSAGE

That God wants to drape wildflowers around my neck, even in the hardest of places, moves me deeply. I carry this truth about in a pocket of my soul, pulling it out like a child with a secret hoarded treasure, longing for the delight David experienced when he wrote those lines. Those are not the words of a man consumed by worry, even though villains and threats of destruction and near misses constantly plagued him.

Last month, my friend the artist sent a birthday card with an invitation to get together to celebrate. We penciled it in for four weeks out. Yesterday, the day we'd reserved, I felt very un-celebratory. My desk, as usual, spilled over with scraps of paper and splayed file folders, to-do lists and urgent messages to myself. Celebrating did not seem affordable in Jane's bomb-site office with its out-of-control time-management issues.

But my artist friend and I have known each other for thirteen years, and God always meets with us when we get together. So talking myself out of anxiety, I played hooky from work and we ate, drank coffee, laughed, and shared stories in my family room. In my kitchen, we examined an exhausted, plate-sized sunflower picked up at the farmer's market the week before. It was a masterpiece, too intricate to add to the compost pile. It seemed disrespectful of such a magnificent piece of art to bury it beneath decomposing organic matter, so I saved it to show my artist friend. The rich brown face of the flower was almost velvety, with yellow tips like the heads of a million pins. We marveled over the plush center, petted the long, wilted petals. What a creation.

I noticed something then. It's hard to worry when studying such carefully orchestrated beauty, when taking a day away from worry just to play.

I told my friend about a nearby field, where seven acres of sunflowers stand at attention with their happy faces. On my last trip past there, I saw a short sign: SUNFLOWERS. In tiny hand-printing, it said, FOR SALE with a wobbly arrow. When we left my home for lunch, my artist friend and I rerouted our trip and pulled into the old farmyard. A woman materialized at the creaking screen door.

"How much are your sunflowers?" we asked after exchanging greetings.

"A dollar each or five dollars a dozen."

My artist friend requested a dozen stems for us to share. The woman headed back inside for boots, a long-sleeved shirt, and shears. When she reappeared, we trudged after her to the field, where she plowed through the giant stems with their golden heads angled toward the morning sun. She wrestled and pulled and hacked with her monster scissors, the flowers shimmying on their stalks. She emerged with an armload of glory. "I snipped sixteen for you," she said, with a smile that would melt ice cubes, as though nothing made her happier than to share those flowers with us.

The stems fill an antique pitcher on my dining room table (my artist friend surprised me with the entire bouquet) and remind me about the rule of play. Sometimes, we just have to quit work and pick flowers with a friend.

I headed back to my desk, tired but happy, not feeling guilty in the least for missing most of the day's work. In my inbox, from people I didn't know, were more emails about speaking. The tool—and rule—of play created an opportunity for God to show off.

My heart flipped over again. It's true. It's really true. As St. Vincent de Paul said, "Those who are in a hurry delay the things of God." By hurrying through my days, chained to my worries, I was delaying the work of God. And come to find out, Jesus was working all along, even when my artist friend and I were playing. Maybe there is something to this, after all. I danced about my office (carefully, mindful of the piles) in delight. This God who throws garlands of wildflowers around our necks . . . this God really does want to meet our needs.

All of them. And sometimes, along the way, like a toddler waist-high in wonder, we just need to shove away from our worry stations. We need to play among the flowers.

The sunflowers are my witness. And God's.

Consider the Wildflowers

If they are not seen, how can you be convinced that they exist?
Well, where do these things that you see come from, if not from one whom you cannot see?
Yes, of course you see something in order to believe something,
and from what you can see to believe what you cannot see.
Please do not be ungrateful to the one who made you able to see;
this is why you are able to believe what you are not yet able to see.
God gave you eyes in your head, reason in your heart.
Arouse the reason in your heart,
get the inner inhabitant behind your inner eyes on his feet,
let him take you to his windows,
let him inspect God's creation.[1]

—Augustine

✻

You can be sure that God will take care of everything you need, his generosity exceeding even yours in the glory that pours from Jesus. Our God and Father abounds in glory that just pours out into eternity. Yes. . . . Receive and experience the amazing grace of the Master, Jesus Christ, deep, deep within yourselves.

Philippians 4:19–20, 23 THE MESSAGE

1. What memories do you have of a tulip-dance season in your life? When did that dance of innocence and delight disappear, to be replaced with worry? When do your needs most hit you? How do you respond? How do you even define needs? When you consider Philippians 4:19–20, what comes to mind? What's missing in your list?

2. How much space and attention does worry occupy in your mind? Go back to the passage in Philippians. What don't you believe?

3. What is your version of the "Take Jesus to Work" dilemma? How do you invite Christ to help you through the long lists filling your life?

4. What about the wildflowers, those play places where you experience God's delight . . . in you? Where are they, what are they? How can you move there, to begin to replace worry with delight? What will play look like for you, today?

~ *Votum* ~

God, I take to the windows.
I see around me, all around,
A panoramic picture
Of your delight, your creativity,
Your playfulness
Your love.

34

For *me*?
For why else have you created such
Vibrant brilliant life
If not because of your delight in
Beauty and
Your delight . . . in me?
I see. And my heart responds.
Like counting petals on a flower. Except
These petals all say
He loves me.
He loves me.
He loves me.
I hold out my hands like a child
Reaching for a bouquet
And you fill me
With yourself.

Benedictus

Sweet Girl,
How I delight in seeing your delight
How I love to surprise you
With the gift of sunflowers
In your work-worried life
Let me come alongside you
Let me carry the load for the moment
Trust me, little one.
Your needs will never overwhelm me.
I long to supply all your needs
To pour out glory and grace
For you.
Just trade me one of your worries
For one of my sunflowers
And see if I don't surprise you
With an entire bouquet.
Today take a moment to play
While I take your worries away.

2

Wearing Red Shoes: Trading Worry for Whimsy

The Tool of Nurture

How worry works . . . and doesn't.
Is it even possible to be tightly tied in with the God
who delights . . . in us?

The shoes were ridiculous. They made no sense in my serious, microphone-wielding, dress-up world, and even less sense in my home office, where I wear thick socks to stay warm in winter and bare feet in summer. No way could I justify those red pseudo-suede look-alike Keds as a necessary expense. But I loved them instantly, was drawn to them like a hummingbird to a brilliant red hibiscus.

Scanning the outlet racks, I found only one pair in my size and held them as though weighing fruit at the grocery. They felt more magical than Dorothy's red shoes, more inviting than her field of red poppies, which says a great deal, all things considered. These tennies felt like childhood, and freedom. Like vacation, and bike riding. They felt like life, and delight.

And a total splurge. The $19.99 price was exactly $19.99 more than I had for fun money. Still, I loved the half-moon beige toes, the matching beige laces and rims, the flat bottoms that reminded me of grade school and junior high, where tennis shoes still meant play in spite of those horrific experiences in gym suits and locker rooms.

My soul responded to the sheer whimsy of those red shoes.

Then my worried left brain forced a look at my watch, snapped me back to adulthood and responsibility. *Gotta run. You don't need those shoes. The warehouse grocery store is calling. Your list is long.*

I grimaced. Warehouse grocery stores rank near the top of my greatest dislike list. With a sassy internal salute to my left brain, I clamped down on the wistfulness, hid the tennies behind a pile of shoes the size of teaspoons, and stomped from the store. I left the shoes, but they didn't leave me. The fun of those shoes worked on my worried soul.

That weekend, I flew to Kansas to keynote a women's conference. My hostess told me about buying a pink dress for her granddaughter; afterward, bag in hand, they wandered down the shoe aisle of the department store.

"Oh, Grandma, I *love love love* those shoes."

My friend looked at her granddaughter's eager face and smiled, then glanced at the object of her affection. Red shoes. *Red* shoes?

"Those are beautiful. But I can't get them for you. They won't go with your new pink dress."

"Oh, please, please, please, Grandma. Why can't I have them?"

"Now, we're not going to whine. You can't have them and that's final."

She dropped off her sobbing, pitiful grandchild and headed home. But this devoted grandmother couldn't banish the tears and pleading from her mind. Finally, after several hours, she capitulated, drove back to the store, and purchased the shoes. The next day, she delivered them to her granddaughter.

The six-year-old yelped. She jumped up and down. She clapped her hands and spun in circles. She took the box in her small hands, held it to her chest. "Oh, Grandma, thank you. Oh, thank you! I love them."

I recognized myself in that six-year-old's dance. But I wasn't sure I recognized God.

Maybe this little dilemma isn't really about being a tightwad, though I am practically certified. I move beyond frugal and thrifty. Rather, I think we have some brutal hallway monitor in our souls who tells us what we should and shouldn't do, or have, or be. How we should or shouldn't act. What we should or shouldn't need. If we listen to that hall monitor, we will be safe, our inner rules tell us.

And there is, after all, something virtuous about worry, about carrying that weight on the shoulders of our soul. Maybe we feel important, or godly, or like we are really paying attention in class, and we really care.

But the statistics about worry tell us that worry drags us to the grim reaper, or at least the doctor or counselor. And worry sure doesn't bring us closer to God.

To say yes to instances of delight, low-cost encounters with something that removes us from the realm of worry and lands us in God's presence, surely can't be wrong. We aren't, after all, talking about buying a yacht or flying to Venice for a cup of espresso. What, after all, is virtuous about denying delight and instead, worrying? Do we have a right to delight? It's not in the Declaration of Independence or in the Bill of Rights.

Delight is not a big line item in the budget of life. It costs very little yet weighs a great deal in terms of benefits. But it so rarely appears on the balance sheet at all. No, my issue—whether delight looks like red shoes or a red lollipop or a redbird—appears deeply rooted in my belief system. Is it possible that God would love to give *me* something red, a dose of delight? Surely God loves me at least as much as the doting grandmother loves her impish grandchild.

Back at home, after I returned, my sticky-note friend wondered about the possibility of my disconnecting from work, playing a little more.

"Oh, when I'm home on Sundays, *if* I'm home, I try not to work. I don't turn on my computer, and I just hang out. But honestly? I get bored." I jiggled my foot, like the kid long ago who gulped down her food so she could get outside and play. But I wasn't playing now, I was just impatient. I didn't want to talk about Sabbath stuff. It's trite and overworked and . . . under-practiced. I didn't even notice until later that she hadn't mentioned Sabbath or Sunday or even rest.

"You have such strict definitions for your life, Jane," my friend said. "For me, not working means listening to my heart. I allow that little girl inside to be set free. So I ask her, 'What do you want to do today?' Sometimes it's pick flowers, or take a nap. Or I realize, 'Ooh, she wants to go get some new slacks.' And then, 'No, it's shoes she wants,' and off we go. Sometimes I turn in a dozen different directions until I hear my own heart."

Shoes? My spirit perked up, like a little girl eavesdropping on an adult conversation about her. I remembered my Kansas friend's story about her granddaughter, then my brain skittered back to the outlet store. I bounced even further back, to childhood. Shoes always slid around on my narrow feet, and finding shoes became one of my mother's hobbies. Even after I was married, she said, "We owe you so many pairs, for all those years we couldn't find shoes that fit."

Well, she actually did a very good job. I only remember a couple of cool teenagers making fun of my sandals when I was an emaciated eleven years old. I'm sure my mother tried to confiscate those loose-soled sandals that flapped apart when I walked, and I dug them out of the trash. I never went barefoot to school or to church and had the requisite two pairs of shoes: school shoes and play shoes.

Play shoes meant Keds, the next must-have after outgrowing our Red Ball Jets. No one I knew had running shoes in those days. Just flat canvas shoes with very little padding. Play had not yet gotten super-scientific or expensive. No air pillows for protection and maximum loft when jumping or pounding down a court. We just stuffed our soles into our shoes and took off as fast as our feet could move.

But play shoes now? My running shoes don't count, because they represent work and obligation, not play. (No one told me that after age eighteen our metabolism grinds to a halt and then starts running in reverse.) In the store the previous week, deliberating over the suede shoes, my pragmatic side had shaken its head with a firm no. Any number of excuses: the money, the impracticality—you can't exercise in shoes without proper cushioning, *and* conscientious women exercise—the "want vs. need" argument. But the ultimate answer was no. I pouted but went on with life.

Really, it's silly that buying red shoes was such a big deal. I considered that. Though a few might frown at such frippery or even call it "un-spirituality," lots of women in my audiences would never think twice about buying the shoes. They would carry them home without a second's hesitation. Further, for many in our culture, our value seems to come from what we own and how we look, with our sense of worth based on net worth. Play has come to mean expensive toys and tools, vacations in ritzy resorts, with loans and credit cards to finance our fun.

In my tightwad heart, those definitions never entered the rule book. And no one's advocating running off on some manic spending spree to feel better about ourselves, to feel worthwhile, some modern-day Imelda Marcos with her 3,000 pairs of shoes and a thousand purses. But you'd think I was raised in the Great Depression, where it cost too much to smile. I worry; I work. And part of my soul withers away.

In the deepest of places, I knew this struggle wasn't about red shoes, not really. Whether or not I had red shoes, I had quite a long walk to recover from my rush-and-worry and work-all-day lifestyle. Red shoes or not, play was nowhere in sight. Nor was delight. But worry? Worry was still number one on my playlist.

After my friend's insight—which seems so basic: Listen to your heart and you move toward healing, toward God, toward life, and even delight—I pondered the shoes yet again, and shrugged. I had a list to work, a list that wouldn't get checked off unless I worked it. Then an outlet mailer landed on my dining room table. Buy one pair, get a second pair half off. I rearranged some errands to route myself there, excavated the hidden red shoes. This time I tried them on. They fit! The child I used to be started jumping up and down like my heart was a trampoline.

At the checkout, the cashier said, "Sneakers aren't included in the shoe sale." *Crud*. I still refused to pay $19.99.

In spite of my howling little kid, I returned the shoes to their hiding place and went on with my errands. But at least I noticed her sadness and longing. *"Aren't I worth it? Aren't I?"* she kept insisting. Poor kid. She just doesn't understand the economy of worry.

Three days later, the 25-percent-off coupon came. Back I headed to the store. The hidden red shoes now sported a sale tag in addition to the discount! I left the store practically dancing, the suede-like Keds bouncing along beside me.

They felt extravagant. Interesting that even after all those trips to the store, I wanted to protest or defend their purchase, which presented a deeper layer to all this waffling. Why is it so hard for me to buy something so small? Is it because God said, "I'll meet your needs," but didn't actually in so many words say, "I'll meet your wants, too, sometimes"?

Rich and our kids would have instantly said, "Buy the shoes." My best friends would have said, "Buy the shoes." My mom, my mother-in-law . . . "Honey. Buy the shoes." But I didn't get second opinions and wouldn't have listened anyway.

People in ministry sometimes joke about taking an involuntary vow of poverty when saying yes to God's call. Whether in professional ministry or not, maybe some of us, or all of us, carry about an internal rule that in order to be content with little (like Paul in his Philippians passage) we must forgo delight. Delight smacks of unnecessary, of optional. With this rule, the needs win and the wants lose, and that feels virtuous. We can pat ourselves on the back. We're doing our part for the war effort.

Does delight get complicated by the Law of Diminishing Returns, where we receive less and less delight from similar stimuli and so we need to increase the dosage? Maybe we fear morphing into an indulgent society, if we give in to something like delight. We're afraid of what we'll learn about ourselves, that we have an inner shoe-aholic who takes advantage of others while feeding her overwhelming appetite.

And indulgence quite possibly leads to an overfed, sedentary, luxury-seeking people with high credit card bills and a low work ethic, wanting something for nothing and the more the better. The crash of 2008 just might prove that theory.

But delight isn't costly in the typical dollars-and-cents sense. Delight is costly as we recognize some inner conflicts in our understanding of God, and what that understanding demands of us in relationship.

Maybe our view of God is skewed, the viewfinder cracked and distorted. Day after day and sometimes hourly, I have to remind myself that God is going to take care of us and delight isn't too much to ask of the God who came to give us something so extravagant as abundant life. God is on duty, and on God's watch, I'm going to be okay. We're going to be okay. This niggles me with worry, too, because God's definition of *okay* and mine might differ a wee bit.

The world looks different from heaven's vantage point, and if I can remember that, then my perspective changes on what is and is not worry. I need to recognize that today, it is well with my soul, and tomorrow, well, tomorrow is God's problem. My friend, in order to establish perspective, tells herself, "If the sun rises tomorrow, then what happens today isn't a catastrophe." And if the sun doesn't rise tomorrow, heaven can't be far off. Right?

Forgoing delight is like an emotional vow of poverty, based on a poor understanding of God. Will God love us more if we live our devout and holy life without cracking a smile or having our heart turn somersaults over the sunset or the erratic path of a butterfly?

As though God were a great big Curmudgeon in the Sky, with furrowed brows and a tight fist. This isn't God the Abba-Daddy, this is God the judgmental, finger-pointing, shaming miser.

But looking around, where's the evidence of a God like that on this globe? Enormous generosity blossoms from the earth, drips from heaven, appears at the lip of the world every single morning and every single evening. Unfailingly generous, it seems to me, is this God we love and serve and maybe try to keep a safe distance from. And if that is true—that we need to keep a safe distance from God, because we know the Old Testament story of the ark bearers who reached out a hand to touch the ark when the oxen stumbled, and the men were struck dead on the spot—then refusing to participate in the delight around us might keep us safe. But safe is an oxymoron when we speak of relationship because relationships will ask us to give what we do not have and do what we cannot do, which is to love all the way to the end of our resources, and then love some more. To dredge down, scrape the bottom of our barrel, and then when we're all out, to rely on the love that must come only from God.

The rock tumbler of relationships will demand that we change, the grit smoothing away the sharp edges, so that we become who we were created to be. Without relationships, there is little catharsis for change and growth. Relationships require risk. They are not safe. Isn't this part of the problem, then, because isn't relationship at the root of delight? Relationship with God's creation, with others around us, with the very Author of delight. So if delight is about relationship, and relationships aren't safe, then we protect ourselves by warding off the hazards of delight.

We continue to live impoverished lives. And worry, all the way to the grave.

Relationship swings wide a portal to delight, to real life, to joy, to worship, to plain old happiness. How can that be frivolous? The red shoes cost seven bucks in the end, and they've escorted me for five years. That works out to be .0038 dollars a day. That's—correct my math if I'm wrong—one-third of one cent every day. Even my little tightwad heart can spring for that tab.

Delight isn't determined by a price tag—it needn't be, can't be. If there were a formula for delight, it seems in inverse proportion to the price tag. Delight is simple pleasure: the gasp at a shooting star, the beauty of a child squealing down a hill barefoot on her scooter. Delight is uncomplicated by finances and folderol, and reaches back to that basic place of childlike wonder and freedom. The lightning bug and kick-the-can freedom of childhood.

So to define delight, it seems to me, removes us from a price tag, and for any skinflints in the crowd, whittles away one more excuse.

Still, there always appear to be better uses of the minimal money we have: gas for the car, tuition, new socks (for someone else). Then my Kansas friend comes to mind, that loving grandmother who knew her granddaughter didn't need those red shoes. The child wanted them, longed for them with every hope in her childish little heart. So Grandma bought them.

My husband worries that my inability to buy something like silly shoes for myself stems from a basic belief that I don't deserve them, that I'm not worth them. I don't think that's it. This is really about not wanting to depend on anyone—or anything. Not wanting to *need* red shoes or a dose of delight. Not wanting to—or at least, not believing that I could—trust God or anyone else to take care of me. If I don't need nurture, then I can stay safe.

It's about bare-bones living. And that's what I was. Am. A bag of bones, rattled with worry and without the flesh of faith around me.

Maybe all the worrisome red-shoe instances of my life come from too thin of a sole on the shoes of faith. Too little trust, from a disbelief that God delights in me even more than the grandmother delights in her grandchild.

But here's the truth, for the record: We were designed for nurture—we need nurture for our very survival. And nurture shows up as delight, a surprise in our worry-about-everything lives. Delight is a decision to trust more. Worrying less follows naturally.

This God, my God, your God, waits to meet us with the anticipation of a delighted daddy, holding his arms behind his back and saying, in a singing voice, "I have a surprise for you." This is the same Jesus who said, "Let the little children come to me . . . for the kingdom of God belongs to such as these" (Mark 10:14). The kingdom? Then maybe red shoes aren't hard to receive, after all.

The next weekend, I wore those red shoes when I spoke in Ohio. I actually wore them while wielding a microphone. But first, I wore them as I walked along the shoreline on Lake Erie. They felt as magical as I'd imagined, and I felt like a child again. I wore them as I lay down on the sand with my camera at water level, catching the sunrise illuminating the rippling lake. I leapt from boulder to boulder, crouched over narrow dynamite tunnels in the rock to listen to the wind rush out from the waves below.

While scrambling over the boulders, sensing movement along the shoreline, I stopped, carefully turned. Standing still as a stone, I watched. Just watched—the sun warm on my hair, pungent lake scent tickling my nose. Logs and branches cluttered the bank, with tiny yellow flowers popping up in the sand-filled nooks. Behind the deadwood, a small head with tiny triangle ears peeked out from a hole in the bank. A young fox flashed out into the morning, then raced to the next nearest gap, disappearing. A second pup popped out, then vanished. Little heads continued to peek, hide, peek, hide.

Right there, on a boulder along the shore of Lake Erie, a group of young foxes played peek-a-boo with me. I was entranced. No one else in *the world* saw this spectacle. God and I were the only audience.

The morning play of these kits, safe in their burrow from predators, spoke to my soul in ways only God would understand, and love. That God cared enough to allow me to see that joyful play moves me. Without the red shoes, I'd have stayed in my room and worked before breakfast, missing a significant encounter with Jesus.

Like a percolator, I bounced back to the conference center in my red Keds. After our session, I lost track of how many women said, some of them with a wistful smile, some with serious play-impoverished faces, some with clear approval, "I like your red tennis shoes."

I grinned. "Thanks. They were a gift to the little girl I used to be." We all smiled, then. These women had been in hard places,

places where deep worries cast a funereal bleakness over any possible delight. Places where worry carved ruts down the faces of their souls. That day, no one questioned the wisdom of the gift of red shoes, or the simple longings of the little girls we once were.

Since then, those shoes have trod the hallowed soils of this world, radiating out from Illinois to California and Guatemala and Japan and the Philippines and Mexico and Japan again, to New Hampshire and a wedding in Texas, and a pathway strewn with phenomenal memories and wondrous ministry. That's serious return on the seven-dollar investment in delight. To think of all that wasted worry . . .

Psalm 5:12 reads, "You are famous, God, for welcoming God-seekers, for decking us out in delight" (THE MESSAGE). Like . . . wearing wildflowers on my feet. A little nurture goes a long, long way.

Consider the Wildflowers

Oh God, who has prepared for them that love thee such
    good things as pass human understanding; pour into
    our hearts such love toward thee,
that we, loving thee above all things, may obtain thy
    promises,
which exceed all that we can desire;
through Jesus Christ our Lord. Amen.[1]

—*The Gelasian Sacramentary, Proper 14*

But you'll welcome us with open arms
    when we run for cover to you.
Let the party last all night!
    Stand guard over our celebration.
You are famous, God, for welcoming God-seekers,
    for decking us out in delight.

Psalm 5:11–12 THE MESSAGE

1. What is your version of "play shoes"? Or do you find yourself on the overindulgent end of the spectrum, honestly? What worries you, when you consider delight versus all the needs around you?

2. What are you afraid of? What do you think about the hypothesis that delight is difficult because delight requires trust in relationships? And conversely, worry is simple, because then we don't need to trust?

3. When do you struggle with the thought that God delights in your delight? With allowing yourself the freedom of delight through nurture? How do you handle that, spiritually, theologically? How do you find the median between self-denial and overindulgence? When have you experienced delight canceling worry?

4. Where have you encountered God's delight through creation? Sometimes, others don't understand those delightful "fox encounters." I was afraid to tell anyone at the conference for fear a local would go roust out the foxes because they might steal someone's chickens or teacup dogs. When have you kept those experiences to yourself? What are you really worried about, and why?

Votum

Jesus, Jesus.
Whether it's red shoes or red cheeks,
You want to see me delight in your love.
You long for me to notice
All the ways you love me
All the encounters
Along the way.
To trust you enough
To play.
A little bit,

Just for today.
To live more
So I worry less
Just for today.

Benedictus

Dear One,
I raised the curtain on the day
And the sun rose with it
And I rub my hands together in delight
At all the ways
I want to love you.
I plan to love you.
I hope you'll notice
I hope you'll recognize
How much I love you
Whether it's the chatter of children at the
Bus stop
Or the sturdy wings of the red-tailed hawk
Soaring outside your window
Or the sun trickling through the leaves
Or maybe just the wind fingering
Your hair
I hope you'll notice
and hear me say
Deep down
"I'm just delighted in you."
And that you'll rest
For just a moment
In my nurturing love
And Live more
And worry less
Today.

49

3

The Forget-Me-Not God
The Tool of Memory

What the forgotten packet of seeds teaches us about worry, the selective memory of God, and the miracle of that delightful kind of love.

I had forgotten about that packet of seeds. Then I forgot what I planted in the pot outside. I thought it might be basil, but forgot about that when the seedlings shot a foot toward the sun on scrawny stems and the leaves smelled just plain green. When the plant bloomed into tiny periwinkle blossoms, I remembered.

These long, slender stalks with the pale-blue petals were forget-me-nots.

Ironically, I forgot about these seeds from several years ago, unearthed ultimately from the ruins of my desk. The packet was a gift from the publisher just before they released a book I coauthored, *Stones of Remembrance*. (Get it? Remembrance . . . forget-me-not?) But I can't forget how that book was one of God's miraculous desert provisions for me, for us, during a worry-fraught time. God provided the chance to work with Dr. Lois Evans, and the foray into the lives of little-known, scarcely mentioned women during the Exodus and the settling of the Promised Land.

Still, in spite of the flowers' blooming, I paid little up-close attention to that container on my porch. Until, that is, we expected company. Until the second they arrive, company worries me. I worry that I will be judged, labeled, found inadequate. I used to even worry that they would eat all our food (I know, it's sick. But I'm getting better about that). I worry about not being ready in time. Before our guests arrived, I flew into my normal worried flurry of straightening and even some outright—as in, desperate—cleaning. The last frontier—since a total teardown and rebuild wasn't possible in the remaining forty-five minutes—was to sweep the front porch. Curb appeal, should they actually enter through the front door.

I eyeballed the planters, then the little weathered stepladder with its broken hinge. I had rescued it from the trash, standing it on the porch to hold planters and birdhouses and whatever else I could fit decorously (or not) on its two narrow steps and the top. This day, this company-coming day, I tugged the rickety ladder and miscellaneous decorations and plants aside to make way for the broom.

The planter containing the forget-me-nots found a temporary home closer to the house. Its long stems curtsied as I gripped both sides of the pot and hefted it a few feet away.

Something scratched the inside of my arm while I swept. *Cheap workout shirt,* I thought. *Must have nylon thread.* I swung the broom viciously, with worry-fueled energy, attacking the spider webs in the overhang, formed since our last company visit. More scratching, like someone had left straight pins in my shirt seams.

Feeling the seams, I found small round burrs the size of BBs. Filled with bristles, designed to stick to anything. A duck's behind or a squirrel's belly, a chipmunk's tail or . . . my shirt.

Suddenly I understood the name. These flowers would not be forgotten. They would stick to anyone and anything with texture.

Even in bloom, they replant themselves. Not only would they spring up in improbable places, but we wouldn't forget them. They would cling to us, scratching and irritating until we noticed.

How ingenious. How annoying. How effective. The completeness of God's creation, the clever means of making certain the plant continues to create and recreate, both moved and settled me. Such intricate detail. Just by my noticing, my constant low-grade worry receded. If God cared so much about these flowers' legacy, maybe, just maybe, God had a plan for me, for us.

Once in school, in Germany, I actually finished a book report early in a rare sweep of efficiency. I stashed it away to hand in on the due date.

Three weeks later, my professor asked why he hadn't received the paper. I riffled through my folder, pulling out the sheets in embarrassment. When he returned it, less one letter grade for tardiness, he wrote on the side, underlining heavily, "Jane. This was a week late." The title of the book? *God's Forgetful Pilgrims*.

I guess I qualified.

Unlike those flowers, maybe selective forgetfulness is part of our nature. Maybe that's why God says repeatedly, in so many words, "Forget me not." Or, "Remember me." *Remember* is used over two hundred times in the Scriptures, not including the times God orders us, "Don't forget."

Sometimes there is even the double injunction: "Remember this and never forget" (Deuteronomy 9:7). Don't forget, but remember.

It isn't always apparent why we're supposed to remember, to not forget. Or what incident or intervention we're intended to keep track of, tying a string around the finger of our memory. I remember the things I would be better off forgetting and forget the things that I really, *really need* to remember. What we remember, and what we forget, creates worry, a drag on the wings of delight. Wouldn't it be better to forget the bad memories, hold on to the good ones, and move forward without the dragging effect of pain? Hanging on to hard memories is like pulling a loaded wagon with flat tires. It's impossible to live more today, impossible not to let worries cast a pall over tomorrow.

Like yesterday. I remember the sin from yesterday morning and the shame that tagged along like a loyal homeless mongrel. I forget the exact words from the Scripture I heard in church, but I need to remember it right now to escape the taunting bully-reminder of my failure.

It returns to me as I palm my Bible and turn the thin pages. I remember more than my sin, if only faintly, as a sand sculpture remembers its shape in the wind. I find the verse in Hebrews 10:17: "I will never again remember their sins and lawless deeds" (NLT). When I heard it yesterday, my sin searing my mind, I nearly burst into tears in that church pew. And it doesn't even matter what sin, for me or for you. What matters is what God says about that sin: "I will never again remember."

This mystery of the faith leaves me trembly, like a seventh-grader with too-big teeth and too-thin legs who has just been told about a boy: "He likes you." Which is the same as saying, "He is forgetting your obvious physical problems and likes you anyway." Is forgetting even possible, remotely likely in this world? Like a data bank, we have immediate retrieval and access to who hurt or wronged us when, and how deep the hurt, or the anger, how bitter the memory, and how poisoned our heart. I hang on to hurts and others' sins against me (or against people I love . . . just issuing fair warning) like a life raft, only to realize: I am the one sinking. But the worst are the sins I have committed—the times I failed a child, or my husband, the despair over wounding another by my transgression.

One friend consoled me when I acted from brokenness rather than healing, "But you meant to do good." That is only a temporary salve, and I can easily rub off the ointment of her words. Because truly, I didn't, often don't, mean to do good, and whether I can lay it at the feet of preoccupation or distraction or lack of healing matters not one whit.

But this thing about God remembering no more. What do I do with that truth, even if I don't understand it and can't explain it theologically? It isn't as though God has Alzheimer's disease. I don't know how the God who knows everything and is perfectly holy forgets something as wretched as my sin, or yours. All I know is—sitting there in church that day, hearing this passage again for maybe the hundredth time in my life—that remembering my sin after I've sought forgiveness destroys delight. If worry means we aren't trusting, and my remembering my failures is not trusting, then it is worrying. And worry? Worry separates me from God, who doesn't even remember in the first place. Doesn't hold it against me, not in the least. He receives my repentance and he receives me. Yes, memory looks backward, but also upward, where we can meet Jesus' eyes.

My friend Gwyn, who has traveled a rough, potholed road for the last decade, has made her way to Jesus. Once, when she'd committed some "my bad," she prayed, "Jesus, you're not going to believe what I did this time."

And for a fleeting incredible moment, she saw Jesus.

He threw back his head. And laughed.

And his laughter beckoned her into a place of forgiveness and healing.

She remembers this—when she worries about her future, her inadequacies, her failures—and she marvels at that kind of love.

It isn't as though Jesus doesn't take our sin seriously. How could he not? It landed him on a cross, pierced by spikes, wracked with pain and an abandonment that we cannot fathom. But so complete is his love, so total his forgiveness, that he throws back his head, laughs, and pulls us close. That is what he wants: us, in his arms.

Like once at our son's hockey game, the coach's own son landed in the penalty box. The devastated kid swung his skates on the cold bench, isolated from the play, his face a study in sorrow. His dad sat on the other side of the Plexiglas, watching both the game and his child. As soon as the penalty ran down, he headed to the box. Opening the gate, he pulled his grief-stricken son into his arms.

Relieved to be remembered and rescued and restored, the child skated back onto the ice, worry gone, play resumed.

The danger of forgetting, of being forgotten, is a type of annihilation: I do not exist anymore. Fear of abandonment creeps in. If I am forgotten, is it forever? And if you forget me, what does it say about your feelings for me? Being forgotten is a type of living death, a penalty box with a timer that never runs down.

Then he said, "Jesus, remember me when you come into your Kingdom."

Luke 23:42 NLT

"Forget me not, Jesus . . . when you come into your kingdom."

They hang on their crosses, those thieves, crosses they presumably deserve. One thief mocks Jesus. But the other . . . the other thief recognizes, in spite of Jesus' battered frame, that this One truly is the Son of God. In contrition, hanging there on that cross with the blood draining from his body, his limbs losing feeling, he acknowledges the Christ, his only hope—his only hope is that Jesus remembers him when he gets to heaven, that there is a life beyond this cross. That, when Jesus bursts from the grave and conquers not only sin but death as well—and isn't sin a death, the death of what God intended from those early days in Eden with the scent of creation still fresh and clean and brand-new?—the thief's only hope is that when the Messiah breaks through that barrier erected after the transgression of perfection in Eden and ascends to heaven, he remembers the thief splayed on the cross next door.

As I consider all the ways that I separate myself from others and God, a fire hose of guilt and shame threatens to drown my flimsy soul—for I have failed hugely, failed to love well, failed to forgive, failed to repent, failed people I adore—and this is my only hope, as well, that Jesus remembers me when he comes into his kingdom.

The miracle, the wonder, stills me. Jesus does more than *remember* me. The author of Hebrews must be dancing while writing, "Therefore he is able to save completely those who come to God through him, because he always lives to intercede for them" (7:25). Saved completely, absolutely, totally. It whirs through my soul like an electric current. No matter what has come before in my life—and I remember, and the enemy remembers, too, and tries to dishearten and destroy me over every single memory—Jesus has saved me completely.

But Jesus doesn't stop with that, though it sure seems sufficient, beyond sufficient, far beyond adequate, to me. He lives to intercede for me. He begs before God for me, for my concerns, for my heart and my mistakes. Christ argues my case—his case—before the judge of all the earth.

If that is not enough, Hebrews describes Jesus as "one who has become a priest not on the basis of a regulation as to his ancestry but on the basis of the power of an indestructible life" (7:16).

Indestructible life! Hear that, fragile, frightened little child that I am, that you are, with our wilted-flower, almost-dying, worry-riddled heart. I wait with that reality; let it soak into my soul like water into sunbaked dirt. If Jesus is our priest based on the power of his indestructible life—and if the life of Christ lives within me—then in the most crucial way possible, deep in my soul, I am indestructible.

Indestructible. That seems almost heretical, to put into black and white for the world to witness. But wait. Remember Galatians 2:20: "I have been crucified with Christ and I no longer live, but Christ lives in me. The life I live in the body, I live by faith in the Son of God, who loved me and gave himself for me."

If Christ has an indestructible life, and I live through him, the Christ in me is indestructible.

That explains why we are even alive at all right this minute. Not because we can recite all our verses or look like we have it all together, but because that indestructible life that is God has not abandoned me, or you. All the corridors of months, and years, when we've wandered about alone and slightly or mostly or totally lost, like a toddler in a hedge maze so high she can't even see a chip of blue sky, every second of every day God remembered, accompanied, protected. Kept us alive. (Imagine what a train wreck life would be without that assurance; it's bad enough as it is.)

And when you tell the truth, it has been a rough road, hasn't it? Sometimes, after I tell women stories about some of my own junk, after I've pointed our wasted, forlorn hearts to the God who loves and remembers, they say, "Thank you for being so honest." Because somehow, when they came to know Jesus, they were told, or else believed based on others' wonderful lives, that life would be a beautifully manicured formal garden—that only good things would come their way, like a raise at work and a perfectly loving handsome husband and darling little poster children, a nice house, a late-model car, vibrant health. They believed their besetting sins would no longer beset, that pain and tears would fall away. And even though life has batted them down like cobwebs, these women have kept their disappointments and disillusionment secret, examining them only briefly in the most secret closets of their soul, daring not to tell others of the incongruity in their lives between their salvation and life in this broken world. They keep their sense of failure a secret.

Our journeys prick and poke like burrs, demanding, "Forget me not," and not only that, remember them aloud to others. People need to know the travails and the hope, not just the pretty picture of praise on our dressed-up Sunday moments when we all sit like hothouse flowers in church. In Lamentations, Jeremiah straightens us out honestly: Life is [sometimes] crappy, and we have to tell the truth. But God? Ah, he says, God. It is almost as though Jeremiah takes a deep breath in his memory, filling himself:

> I remember my affliction and my wandering, the bitterness and the gall. I well remember them, and my soul is downcast within me. Yet this I call to mind and therefore I have hope: Because of the Lord's great love we are not consumed.
>
> Lamentations 3:19–22

So to live in the ever-present delight of God, call it to mind. Remember: God's love is from everlasting to everlasting. How can God possibly forget us, God who envisioned us from the dawn of the world and eagerly accompanies us at every turn of our wild ride? God wraps around us like bumpers on a bumper car.

Remembering, God reminds us: Our presence is a miracle. You are a miracle, your sojourn stunning. When I remember the perilous passage to this place called here and now, remember the harrowing near misses and close calls, I shake my head and marvel. When I see our children, and remember their travels and travails to this day and the mistakes and misjudgments I have made as their mother, it's a wonder they are alive. God has saved me from so much, saved them from such misadventures.

And we only know what we can *see*. The real story is much deeper. We cannot know the battles behind the scenes, the near-death experiences, the narrowly avoided traumas in which God intervened, like Superman braced between us and calamity. Imagine heaven, when we sit around and God tells us bedtime stories. "Remember that time, when you were despairing and ready to give up? Want to know how many angels I posted on that shift?" And God laughs, shaking with joy. "Let me tell you *that* story."

This remembering reminds us, loosening the cinch around our heart, making room for delight: We are not an accident, though our expedition through the wilds of this world may seem accidental. And one day we will hear, and remember, and flush with the joy of being cherished and protected.

Sometimes, when I return from a speaking event, someone asks, "Did you have a good trip?" If they asked that about our lives, maybe we would widen our eyes in disbelief. Because in our darkest nights of the soul, we weep and shout and maybe even shake our fists at God. "You have forgotten me," we wail, along with King David, who shook his fist and yelled and wept plenty of times in Scripture. When people we love get caught in the rusty-toothed traps of crisis and consequences, we beat our chest and sob, "Don't forget, God. Don't forget." When we buckle over in pain because it hurts too much to stand, because life is so hard we have to curl over and wrap ourselves tightly together to keep from falling apart, our words throb in rhythm with our heart, "Don't forget, God. Don't leave me here alone."

Remember, though: God's words about not forgetting, about remembering, go further than just our active recounting or discarding of moments in our past. God says, "I will never forget you" (Isaiah 49:15 CEV). That though our mother and father forsake—forget—us, as though that were even remotely possible, because however anguished their experience may be as parents, they cannot forget their children, cannot ignore how their own bodies and hearts have stretched and scarred and grown as a result of their children—that God will take us in (Psalm 27:10). That God, Creator of heaven and earth, the very One who shaped us in our mothers' wombs, God remembers.

All those times you cried yourself to sleep?

God heard, God cared, God wept. God remembered. And God awakened you morning after morning and mourning after mourning, loving you from afar, sending love through eternity to the here and now of your life through people you may not even know or remember. Though we might not remember or even have recognized God's presence, God was present. God is present in all our yesterdays, our todays, our tomorrows.

No matter what, God does not forget us. Cannot forget us—because we are the burr of the forget-me-not stuck to his heart.

I perch on the porch steps. Thrift-store birdhouses and spindly plants in mismatched planters surround me without recrimination. They seem happy to be alive in, and perhaps in spite of, the scorching Midwest heat wave, the hottest since we've been recording the world's temperature. We haven't had company in a while, so the porch needs a broom attack. Cobwebs flourish. Dirt and leaves gather beneath the grayed and battered stepladder like old memories.

Today, I ponder my children when they were toddlers, with their pert funny charming wiry ingenious personalities, their big deep eyes. I grieve the loss of the children they were, the innocence of those early years, and the pain of their days that brings them to now. I worry about their faith, because the way has been hard and the path strewn with briars and boulders. No matter our age, it is sometimes hard to believe God loves us when life is so thorny, when we pray until our hearts bleed themselves dry and still God doesn't seem to answer.

Beside me, peering over a slim butterfly house with a blue roof, the dainty forget-me-not flowers sway in a ballet with the faint breeze. They survived the winter, and now in their second blooming this season, they remind me: God does not forget. And will bring into bloom, into resurrected life, all that has gone before us, scarring and shaping us. God remembers.

Worries flee. Delight hovers, there, on the porch. It looks like the forget-me-not.

Consider the Wildflowers

Remember above all what he has done in Christ—remember those moments in our own lives when with only the dullest understanding but with the sharpest longing we have glimpsed that Christ's kind of life is the only life that matters and that all other kinds of life are riddled with death; remember those moments in our lives when Christ came to us in countless disguises through people who one way or another strengthened us, comforted us, healed us, judged us, by the power of Christ alive within them. All that is the past. All that is what there is to remember. And *because* that is the past, *because* we remember, we have this high and holy hope: that what he has done, he will continue to do, that what he has begun in us and our world, he will in unimaginable ways bring to fullness and fruition.[1]

—Frederick Buechner, *Secrets in the Dark: A Life in Sermons*

I remember my affliction and my wandering, the bitterness
    and the gall.
I well remember them, and my soul is downcast within me.
Yet this I call to mind and therefore I have hope:
Because of the Lord's great love we are not consumed,
for his compassions never fail.
They are new every morning; great is your faithfulness.
I say to myself,
"The Lord is my portion; therefore I will wait for him."
The Lord is good to those whose hope is in him,
to the one who seeks him;
    it is good to wait quietly for the salvation of the Lord.

Lamentations 3:19–26

1. When do you forget about God's presence beside you? When do you drag yesterday's sin into today? How does this impact your worry?

2. To not be remembered feels like annihilation. Describe a time when you begged God to remember, but God was silent. What was that like for you? How fresh is the pain?

3. What do you need to forget, to relinquish? What do you wish God would forget about you, or others would forget? (Because doesn't it seem like others sometimes remember the very worst things about you? And not the best? Or maybe they remember the good stuff and you shake your head, remembering all too well your failures?)

4. Where is a good remembering place for you? What will you call to mind, and therefore have hope? What does this do for your worries?

Votum

Ah, Lord Jesus.
Forget-me-not, there in your Kingdom.
Forget my sins,
Remember your sacrifice
Forget-me-not, Christ.
Remind me of your love
Rescue me from
the unforgettable wraith
of unforgiveness
And the pain I need to forget.
Remember all that worries me
And
Forget
Me
Not.
Because you are my only
Hope.

Benedictus

Dear One!
I cannot forget you
For you are engraved on the palms
Of my hands
And your face and your pain
And your tears and your
Worries are always before me.
And always
I am interceding for you
Infusing my indestructible life—
Death could not keep me!—
Into yours.
Know that I remember
And I ever live to remember
You in heaven
And even now plead your case.
And what was that? That sin
You are remembering?
I have no recollection
But only this
That I love you.
And that should
Do it.
I hope today
That you can hear my laughter
And my love.

4

Boxed In . . .
But Climbing Out

The Tool of Breaking Free

On the entrapping worry-boxes we build
and the wide-open places of God's delight.

In the closing scene of the movie *Breakfast at Tiffany's*, Paul Varjak (George Peppard) and Holly Golightly (Audrey Hepburn) pile into a taxi with her cat.

Paul pulls out a message from Holly's supposed fiancé.

Holly, recognizing bad news, busies herself digging in her purse. Because a girl can't do a thing without wearing lipstick, she bats her huge eyes at Paul and asks him to read the message.

It is bad news. Paul expects her to change her mind about fleeing the country to meet her fiancé in Brazil. She refuses, ordering the taxi driver to head to the airport. Paul tries his final argument. He loves her; she belongs to him.

Holly, who has spent her entire life running away from herself and anyone who said or pretended they loved her, pushes back, refusing to let anyone put her in a cage.

But Paul wants only to love her, not cage her. At this, Holly's voice rises to a wail. She doesn't even know who she is. She's not Holly or Lula Mae, she's as homeless and nameless as her no-name cat.

She pounds on the seat to get the driver's attention, then pushes the cat out the door into the hammering rain.

Paul barely controls his anger, furious that she won't stick out her chin and face the facts: People fall in love; people belong to one another. "Because that's the only chance anybody's got for real happiness. . . . You're terrified somebody's gonna stick you in a cage. Well, baby, you're already in that cage. You've built it yourself. And it's not bounded in the west by Tulip, Texas, or in the east by Somaliland. It's wherever you go. Because no matter where you run, you just end up running into yourself."

Like Holly, we worry that we can't run fast enough to outrun our past and the people who tried to fence us in. Really, perhaps, we are trying to run faster than our failures, to outrun our worries and the risk of more failure. Maybe one of our boxes, the box we find ourselves inhabiting, like Holly Golightly, is one we have built ourselves.

This past week, when our daughter flew home for a visit, we hauled a bin of her left-behind belongings from the attic. Ruthie sorted it into thrift-store offerings versus gifts. The box waits for me to empty the gifts into luggage and cart them along on my next trip.

For now, its lid leans against the translucent storage bin. Because it's been abandoned in front of me for days (which should worry me, but doesn't), I've studied that lid. On the inside of the stark white plastic, a yellow sticker issues a dire visual warning. It depicts the silhouette of a baby sitting in the box with her head above the edge. The lid opens over her at an angle from one end, like a sloped roof. A big red Do-Not circle with a diagonal slash covers the entire diagram, making words unnecessary: Do Not Put a Child in This Box. Presumably, she will suffocate inside.

Unless they intend the pictured warning to mean: Do Not Let the Child's Head Stick Out of the Box. Tuck her in, instead. But no, surely that isn't the meaning of the picture. (Please do not try this at home. Author assumes no responsibility for at-home experiments.)

Looking at the box full of gifts, and the warning with the innocent baby, I wonder about the boxes we've tried to stuff ourselves into, or perhaps those boxes that others have tried to close around us. And even about the possible second interpretation, "Don't stick your neck out." In other words, don't take risks, don't live adventurously; don't do anything where you might get hurt. If the roof of that lean-to falls, you might get brain damage or a broken neck, a concussion, or at least a topknot on your head.

Learning to worry less and live more, learning to live in delight, in the delight of our wild-about-us God, entails identifying the boxes endangering us and the ways we've followed the don't-stick-your-neck-out rule. We may actually be surprised at the gifts stored inside those boxes. And even more surprised when we employ the tool of breaking free.

Sometimes, children need boxes. It sure seems not only helpful but necessary to have a containment principle—allowing a baby to sleep in a bassinet with high soft sides, for instance, for the baby's maximum comfort and safety, and minimum worry for the parent. From there, we graduate to a crib (again, with high sides but more room to roll and flop and eventually rattle and try to scale the side rails) and then to play within the safe confines of a playpen. The principle seems to be one of enlargement: As we grow in curiosity and physical ability and also a sense of safety, our borders expand with our exploratory longings.

It all makes great sense. Eventually, as we near adulthood, the boxes stretch until we are free to make our own choices. But sometimes, we don't know when we've outgrown the boxes, if we even see their parameters any longer. Like Holly, we don't have any idea how to outsmart the cages we've built for ourselves. Especially if, along with the boxes, we've clung to the don't-stick-your-neck-out rule for living and put a lid on ourselves.

Don't stick your neck out is a recipe for caution, for low-risk living. Worry and fear create a cautious child—one who will never try to peer out of her box or spring the door on her cage. It seems far more dangerous than inviting a child into common sense. Caution—not to be traded for foolishness—stifles delight when it rises from fear, when it originates with worry about making a mistake, failing, being hurt by another, or not being liked. If we worry about others' impression of us, we might never get out of our box. We may never stick our necks out.

Worry is next of kin to fear, and fear has been one of my tightest boxes. Fear of being disliked, fear of failing, fear of not being good enough. Fear of abandonment, of arguments, of making mistakes. Fear of dreaming, because this incorporated all the other fears.

All those worry-based fears created a tiny little self-crafted box for what a pastor's wife, or even a Good Christian Woman, should be like. Mostly, my box involved singing hymns and praise songs all day long, smiling a lot and obediently, never being angry, loving everybody, and squelching my personality, which was easy because I forgot I had one while I was trying to live a Serious and Holy Life. Oh, and saying yes to every job and need that cropped up in the church or neighborhood. (I had my limits. I no longer tried to help the entire world.) With all these elements framing my box, I failed miserably. At all of them.

Breaking out of that Holly Golightly cage began, ironically, with my own breakdown in the first church my husband pastored out of seminary. (Funny, my auto-correct just changed that word to "pastured," which is strangely close because we moved out to the pasturelands of western Illinois. And I felt a little set out to pasture, with our home boxed in on one side by the church and cemetery, on two sides by a handful of houses, and on the fourth side, running behind us for miles, the wide open fields.)

In spite of postpartum depression, I yes'd and smiled and pretended myself right into a sullen, ugly clod of humanity, silencing my anger over both valid and ridiculous issues because Good Christian Women don't get angry. The breakdown was the best impetus I'd ever had to becoming myself, to begin to listen to the plaintive little girl inside who dreamed dreams in fourth grade that she'd never voiced aloud to anyone. Gifts in the box? It never occurred to me they might be mine.

Somehow, I missed the lesson on dreaming. I don't remember tests to determine our gifts and inclinations, nor guidance counselors meeting with each student individually to ascertain our direction once we neared the rim of the box that was high school. My friends were all heading to college to be teachers, and not just ordinary teachers: special education teachers. Because I thought I had to be like everyone else, and this must be what good Christians should do, I decided I should, as well. My parents were very quiet when I mentioned this secondhand dream, wisely so.

That borrowed dream didn't make it past high school graduation. After years of sewing and exhibiting in 4-H fairs, I left high school and landed in fashion merchandising for a major, then switched universities for a BS in business. Even though in high school I had to be tutored through pre-algebra and got diarrhea before every higher math exam, even though I was so quiet I could barely put a sentence together unless I knew you well, this somehow seemed sensible, something that should get me a job if I could work up the courage to figure out what that job might be.

So many signings in my junior high and high school yearbooks say, "To a nice, sweet girl" (or sometimes, "To a nice sweat girl").

My nice-sweet-girl personality masked a shyness and a fear that didn't allow much in the imagination department, but God rattled my cage as a college junior, and I walked blindly into plans I couldn't have hoped for, wouldn't have dared stick my neck out to achieve because they were so far beyond the realm of the possible or plausible.

They were so gradual I didn't realize where they'd lead, nor did I recognize the gentle and insistent hand of God preparing me for the future. For a dream returned, one that I had forgotten I'd dreamed as a crayon-thin, trying-to-be-obedient little girl, with big eyes, sitting at a scarred wooden desk with its gulley for pencils and a lift-up top. The classroom I would have given anything to stay in for fifth grade too, except that kind Mrs. Hall only taught fourth.

Probably also a good thing I didn't discern where God had covertly pulled me. I would have screamed in terror and married the first person I could find who would keep me safe and never expect that I become a more complete me.

Still, back in the early days of pastoral ministry, to have actually confessed or confided in my husband—let alone any other living soul—that I wanted to be a writer? It seemed like a dream only important, bright people with a significant background in college writing courses could entertain, people born of impact-makers, famous writers, thinkers. We do not come from dreaming stock (my family of origin)—at least I didn't think we did at the time. Hardworking, entrepreneurial, yes. Funny, bright, quick, yes. (But now I realize that my parents and both sets of grandparents, while trying to make a living for their children, did indeed exercise the art of dreaming. One grandfather started a construction business on a dream and a few nickels and managed to scrape together enough buffalo heads to buy a single piece of equipment. He and my grandmother parked this under a tree and set up shop. Seems like dreaming and risk taking, especially in a postwar America where people had enthusiasm but also a lot of wounds.)

As far as I know, though, no artists, writers, actors, or musicians hang from my family tree. To consider branching out onto that kind of limb from the good Christian girl and circumspect pastor's wife I was trying to be felt both far-fetched and foolish, to say nothing of risky. That worry, I flat-out refused to entertain.

But when our boxes become cement walls that prohibit dreaming, we start to die, even if we don't notice the rigor mortis for years. It's never too late to get out of the box—unless it's made of pinewood.

Sometimes, it's just easier to put a lid on it all, shushing ourselves. Sound waves disturb others.

Sometimes we really have to shush ourselves, or another—at church, a funeral, or some other solemn ceremony where it's just not about us. But sometimes, ad campaigns and slogans notwithstanding, it is about us. And at those times, rather than meaning "Don't be loud or inappropriate," doesn't "Put a lid on it" really mean "Please, please, please contain your colorful personality"? Or, please don't make my life more difficult by being different than I am, or creating a scene? Don't embarrass me? And, even more dangerous: Please don't climb out of your box and stick your neck out and remind me that I have stopped dreaming or can't afford to dream? Because if everyone contains—or cages—both self and one another, we are all safely boxed in (like the Stepford Wives—such a very happy group of women).

I put a lid on myself because of my own insecurities. I so muffled my voice that I didn't know I had one—I didn't realize I had opinions. I didn't want to be wrong, I didn't want to disagree. The bottom line, for me, was that I didn't want any arguments or conflict because I wanted people to like me. To be happy. It was easier, or seemed smarter, not to think and not to question.

It's been hard to bust out of the put-a-lid-on-it rule, and the don't-stick-your-neck-out rule as well. In college, my friend Karen and I prepared to lead a Bible study with a group of really smart co-eds, some of whom had led very involved and well-researched studies I'd attended. Karen and I both contributed equally to the preparation and then decided who would lead which section of the study. On D-Day (as in, delivery day, the day of the study, or even, disaster day), Karen opened the study, and then waited for me to speak.

I could not unlock my jaws. The guy who knew Greek was there. The grad student who led a parachurch group lounged on a nearby patch of carpet. Even though I had been in musicals with hundreds of people watching, I now stared mutely at the piece I was to deliver. My cheeks felt feverish. I knew my ears were getting red because they felt like they would ignite.

Karen rustled the paper and pointed to my part, and looked increasingly nervous. I widened my eyes and shook my head, mortified. Worse than Moses, I couldn't even stutter out my part. She led the entire session.

Funny. I have felt embarrassed and ashamed of this for years. Recently I caught up with my college friend and asked her about that time. She didn't remember my failure at all.

But failure isn't necessarily a sign that we shouldn't try to climb out. Because our failure is irrelevant to God's calling. Turns out, both the memory of failure and the God who rattles cages, setting prisoners free, the God who shods them in red shoes, were leading the way.

Given my worries and fears and opinion-less approach to relationships and life, what a surprise when I started writing and then speaking, to realize that I not only had thoughts and opinions—but people were willing to publish them for thousands of readers, and were even paying me to voice them. But the ratification of others, the power others have to put a lid on us, is still active today. There is a box in Christianity that says exercise your gifts, but only if everyone agrees that you can. Once I was the first woman invited to speak at a denomination's national gathering. When the board voted to invite me, the single dissenting vote arose from a man who said, "Okay, then, I can skip that session."

The directors refused to allow him to miss what God might say through this unlikely vessel. But God speaks through donkeys and dreams, and I was somewhere in between.

Like I said, my dreams appeared seemingly from nowhere, unexpected to me and everyone who knew me. Once, when childhood friends began appearing on Facebook, I posted an invitation to visit a church near my hometown, where I would be speaking. One woman wrote on my wall, "I'd love to come hear what the quiet girl from high school has to say."

The fear box, it seems, for me and maybe for others, is really a box within a box, like those nesting dolls that come apart in the middle. In the hollow of the first one, another doll hides, and inside that, another one, and another, until you finally reach the very core, a tiny baby of a doll.

I put a lid on myself, my reactions, tears, childlikeness, gifts, and opinions, because in one box I feared rejection. But the box inside that box was about abandonment—I will be left alone if I am truly myself. And within that box: the certainty that I was not worth loving, that no one could really love me, the real me.

Especially not God, the God who knows all and sees all and is absolutely holy. He couldn't have any patience with me, couldn't possibly love me. To consider that God might delight in me never once crossed my unimaginative, unexplored mind. Like Holly Golightly, no matter where I went, I stayed in my box and kept running into myself.

But after that breakdown in our first parsonage, our first real-life experiment of ministry after seminary, my wrestling match began. The dialogue with myself went something like this:

Do I believe God loves me?

Yes. [Long pause.] *No. Not really. Not deep down.*

The good pastor's wife doesn't believe God loves her?

No. Not really.

When I imagine myself as a child, admitting this, I barely lift my chin, can barely see out beneath my pixie bangs. The summer freckles twitch and my lips form a wistful half-smile, a smile that apologizes for such a significant failing.

I would like to tell you that the wrestling match ended with a never-doubting sense of God's love for me. That ever since, I have lived with a constant awareness that the Creator of the heavens and the earth and the galaxies and the six million leaves on the maple tree outside my window and the 228 working muscles in a caterpillar's head . . . that this God loves me, loves me. Loves. *Me.*

But that would be a lie, and I'm trying not to be a liar. I don't always live there.

Here's what I know: In the Scriptures, the couplet "unfailing love" never occurs in the context of a man's love for a woman, a parent's for a child, a friend's for a friend. But always in the way God cares about us. Unfailing. Love. God is unfailing; God's love is unfailing. God loves, unfailingly.

This surprises me, still, after years of fears, after boxes inside boxes with lids on them to keep me safe. And the places where I experience that love surprise me, as well. When I watch the leaves clapping their hands in mysterious rustling. When I see a baby bunny with a brilliant orange blossom of the trumpet vine in its mouth, as though playing it. When the sun reflects off water, a bouncing ball of glory that splashes like a bubble over me. When I speak in front of groups, I am so conscious of God's love that I could jump, cry, and laugh.

Sometimes I just pray, "God, would you show me you love me?"

One of my kids, taller than me, sometimes sneaks up behind me and traps my arms, then blows raspberries on my neck until I collapse, shrieking in laughter.

And I think, really, that God is like that. Blowing a raspberry on my neck. Flashing a hummingbird past my window. Showing me the half shell of a robin's egg.

The cage I have built for myself, the box I've lived in so long, springs open, and I break free of my fear of failure and being unloved. I flutter out. Delighted in. And delighted.

Consider the Wildflowers

Just these two words He spoke
changed my life,
"Enjoy Me."
What a burden I thought I was to carry—
a crucifix, as did He.
Love once said to me, "I know a song,
would you like to hear it?"
And laughter came from every brick in the street
and from every pore
in the sky.
After a night of prayer, He
changed my life when
He sang,
"Enjoy Me."[1]

—Saint Teresa of Avila

74

He stood me up on a wide-open field;
I stood there saved—surprised to be loved! (THE MESSAGE)

He brought me out into a spacious place;
he rescued me because he delighted in me.

He led me to a place of safety;
he rescued me because he delights in me. (NLT)

Psalm 18:19

1. What boxes did you grow up in? Where are your boxes now, and when do you recognize them? In what ways do your friends or others put you in a cage? How is worry one of your boxes?

2. When are you afraid to stick your neck out? Why? What is the root of that fear? What are you really worried about? And what about your core fear, that innermost nesting box?

3. How do you experience the unfailing love God has for you? How can you wait for that love to appear, each day, so you can live in delight a little more often, for a little longer? What does this do to your worry levels?

4. Where have you experienced breaking free? Where do you need or want to break free? How will you risk that?

Votum

Unfailing God, this box constricts me.
I want to go lightly through this day,
Through this life, this world.
I do not want to live hindered by fears
Of abandonment, of failure, of rejection
Of not being loved.
Today, I wait with you, knowing in my brain
That you love me.
Hoping to experience that love

In my soul.
I want to break free,
To flutter and spin, God
To worry less and live more in your loving delight
Made new every day
Because . . . you love me.

Benedictus

Hello, Daughter-o'-Mine!
How delighted I am
That those boxes cannot contain you
Any longer
That you are breaking free and breaking out
Of the cages others—and you yourself—have
Built around you.
There are gifts within that you will love
To open and to use in this world
You can worry about what other people think
Or whether you will fail
Or you can embrace what I think of you.
Keep sticking your neck out
And trusting me
Allow me to place you in the wide-open
Spaces of my love.

5

Bread of the Presence
The Tool of Constancy

Worry, homemade bread, and the dailyness of the presence of God.

The bread machine agitated on top of the portable dishwasher, kneading the dough for me, and then settled down to bake its contents into a gorgeous golden loaf of bread. It rose with a perfect arch, a wholesome throwback to simpler times. Fresh bread, five ingredients, better than a gong calling everyone to dinner. Even the dog stood outside the screen door, tail wagging, smiling her dolphin-faced grin, when I placed the hot bread on the slotted cutting board and swathed it in a fresh cloth.

Is there anything more inviting than a loaf of homemade bread, fresh from the oven, a butter dish nearby waiting to pour itself in a benediction over the hot loaf? The bread told those circling the table, "You are special. Someone cared enough about you to plan this meal hours earlier, and then to time it precisely for your appearance."

At least, that's what I hope it meant. Friends and relatives always looked for a hot loaf of bread on the dinner table, and the children's cohorts couldn't get enough of the delicacy. One friend found herself a bread machine and studied it anxiously, worried that the bread wouldn't taste like mine. Now these are not tricky appliances and are very forgiving. I have no magic touch. But still, she asked, "Can you teach me how to do this?" and then later, a few loaves later, "Wait, can I watch you? Let me write this down."

The kids overheard and teased me for years. They'd seen my splattered recipes and knew how easy the task. "You should star in a television show, *Baking Bread with Jane*."

One day, after about a million dances on the countertop, the bread machine danced itself right over the edge and crashed, putting an end to the homemade bread era in our lives. By then, bread was on my forbidden list, the gluten tearing down my insides. And by then the kids were scattered around the country, their friends' legs no longer stretching beneath our table; our table gatherings shrunk to two, and our meals simplified.

I gulp around the logjam in my throat. Sometimes I smell bread baking and understand the adage, "For a loaf of bread a man will steal." Or at the very least, dance a jig of delight.

Bread is like a homemade greeting card that reads, "I care. I remember you. I think of you, and I think this will delight you." This substance we "taste and see," and affirm deep in our gustatory souls the psalmist's words, "The Lord is good" (Psalm 34:8). The bread of remembrance. Isn't that what Jesus is speaking of, breaking the bread? "This is my body given for you; do this in remembrance of me" (Luke 22:19)? Isn't bread a symbol of the very dailyness of faith, the dailyness of a faithful God? Bread from heaven, the sign in the wilderness that God would carry his people through, that God would lead and feed them all the way to the Promised Land? Bread represents a daily promise of faithfulness.

Bread is a mnemonic device, a remembering tool, and every time we "eat this bread," we can remember. Every time, not just on the fifth Sunday or the first Sunday or during the weekly service of Communion, or Wednesday Eucharist. Always, when we eat, we remember God's dailyness. Remember that somehow, God fed us yesterday. God is feeding us today. And God will feed us tomorrow.

In our current economy, we've entered into times when food for today or tomorrow may not be assured. So many people hang over the lip of a cliff. Maybe not sure that tomorrow is a guarantee, at least not of food, or even a home to live in. So easy to worry, the default setting on our faithless spin cycle.

And worry becomes fear, the dividing line blurring until the morphing is complete. It's no surprise that people get into fistfights for a crust of bread. Hunger reminds us of our very fragile existence, and the internal clawing of hunger pain—or the fear that we will one day, sooner or later, be hungry—turns us desperate. Current hunger—whether literal hunger or hunger for safety, or approval, or relationship—makes it easy to forget that so far in our lives, we've managed to get by on the food God has provided, one way or another.

Once a week, at least, observant Jews lift the bread at the table and remember God's provision. Today we are okay, and tomorrow is in God's hands. But not me. I borrow the tomorrows for today, and store them in my worry trough, and the age-old fears creep back into my sleeping dreams and my waking worries.

But it's an exhausting lifestyle, this paddling of worry, like the agitator in the bread machine never turning off, and my short-term memory—my long-term memory, for that matter—deficient. Although I actually don't worry about tomorrow's provisions, not so long as there's food in the cupboard. No, I worry about three months from now, when maybe we're down to the last crust of bread, when Mother Hubbard's cupboards are bare, and her fridge and deep freeze and spare pantry, too. To say nothing of her savings account and home equity loan.

It's never happened, but just the same, maybe by worrying I'll be prepared for the worst.

My artist friend called one day. She'd stumbled onto a treasure trove of expensive gluten-free breads, free. Would I be offended if she got them for me?

Offended? I've never been offended by free. I love free. I especially love free when it comes to bread, and I love free even more with two of my kids (probably three, but one remains irritatingly undiagnosed) bearing the same disease. How I love to offer them bread that nourishes rather than destroys.

And so even this week, as I've gnawed and nibbled the bread of worry rather than faith, my sweet friend called. "I have bread in the freezer. Shall we . . . ?" and we planned a lovely quiet day, half of it spent in personal retreat, half of it spent over a birthday meal, and ending at her house, with my cooler ready for a freezer-full of special breads.

Daily bread.

Last week, I perched on the edge of a bed in our guest room, the room that was our daughter's before she moved out of state for college and her adult life, and then our son's when he boomeranged home for a season. A collage of pictures sits atop the bookshelf. His name means, "God remembers," and I looked at him, his one-year-old face smeared with chocolate cake at his birthday, his eyes rich and deep and gleaming. In another, he sleeps curled up in a small wagon being towed by his grandfather. Next to that photo, he stands with his best buddies in their prom tuxedos. In another, he hoists a championship hockey stick in the air, handsome and heartbreaking with his luminous smile.

Without planning, I began to recite the Lord's Prayer for him. ". . . Thy will be done, on earth as it is in heaven. . . ." Daily bread. Deliver him from evil.

Now, throughout my own days, I find myself praying the Lord's Prayer. Daily bread. Thy will be done. The prayer reminds me to be watching for that daily bread, for the dailyness of God's faithfulness, for the provisions that show me God is watching out for me, for those I love. But I also find that this discipline, this praying deliberately the prayer Jesus taught us to pray, does more than just tamp down my worries. This prayer totally redirects my gaze, away from worry and fear, and toward the One who provides.

God's supplies for God's people jam-pack the Scriptures. The stuff of legends, of stories handed down for thousands of years. Heavens that rain bread, like the book *Cloudy With a Chance of Meatballs,* a graphic picture of God's faithfulness. Bread, the picture of the dailyness of God's tending. *The Lore of God's Love.* That could be the title of an epic romance. The romance of bread, of Bread, fresh from the Baker's hand. The wooing by the God who loved us enough to give us . . . the Bread of heaven, nourishment not just for today for our stomachs, but for forever, for our souls.

Bread throughout the Scriptures is a sign of God's overseeing love, love that provides food for both body and soul. It is a symbol of faith. It is delight, inhaled, ingested. It is the panacea for worry, this dailyness of God's offerings to us.

Bread shows up early in the Bible, as a sign of hospitality. Melchizedek, king of Salem, offered bread and wine to Abram after a vivid and impressive victory against the enemy kings who had kidnapped his nephew Lot (Genesis 14). Then Abram got his new name, and when God visited him and his wife at their tent, Abraham rushed Sarah into preparing bread for the honored guests, one of whom turned out to be God.

And the lure of grandson Jacob's bread, warm, wafting its way into his twin brother Esau's senses, caused Esau to lose his sense and also his birthright as Isaac's firstborn son. Double-tricking Jacob continued his relationship with bread after baking it for Esau to accompany the stew and worming his way into his unrightful inheritance—his own son Joseph interpreted the baker's dream of bread while exiled in Egypt (Genesis 40:16). This won Joseph exactly zero popularity contests. But the interpretation of the dream about bread eventually brought his lost family down to Egypt and saved their lives because Joseph had stockpiled grains to make bread while rising (pun intended) to the second-highest position in Egypt.

Bread. Four hundred years later, after the Israelites fell from favor and became slaves instead of guests in Egypt, God told them to make bread without yeast, instituting the Feast of Unleavened Bread (not to be confused with Passover, when death passed over the homes of the Israelites who smeared lamb's blood over their doorposts). They packed their bags with the life-saving substance of bread, made in a hurry without yeast, sustenance critical for the journey out of slavery in Egypt and through the wilderness.

But when the Israelites escaped their bondage, they ran out of bread within six weeks. And they whined. They reinvented their past and pretended that they had all the bread they wanted in Egypt, where they were mighty skinny slaves if you watch *The Prince of Egypt* version of the story. (See Exodus 16.) I doubt they ate all the bread they wanted, "bread to the full" (v. 3 NKJV), but memory is a tricky device when hunger renders you wan, weak, and hopeless. The past looks good and the future looks fatal, seen from worry-filled eyes.

Even as their *kvetching* (griping) steamed its way toward heaven, God said, "I'm going to rain bread down from the skies for you. The people will go out and gather each day's ration. . . . and you'll realize that I am God, *your* God" (Exodus 16:4, 11 THE MESSAGE). And the people gathered the bread each morning and witnessed the glory of God, of God's provision for them, in the manna, the "What is this?" that fell like the dew and covered the ground.

They watched for that bread every single day for nearly forty years (minus the first six weeks, when they ran out of their own resources and resourcefulness). On the sixth day of all two-thousand-plus weeks in the wilderness, they were to gather double the amount of bread, and in that way demonstrate to God that they trusted him to care for them while they rested. If God provided bread all week long, then surely God had day seven covered.

They probably worried anyway, especially as they hit the banks of the Promised Land, because it's easy to forget who's in charge of the food when we're the ones doing the tilling and hoeing and weeding and planting and grinding. And now that we are so far removed from agriculture, some children haven't the faintest concept of farming—seed, grain, harvest—all leading up to bread on their table purchased from a convenience store in a nice plastic bag. All these years after the bread in the wilderness, we still believe bread comes from our own work. We forget, thus we worry. They forgot, and they worried.

God seemed to understand this, because in Exodus 16:31–33, God tells Moses, "Keep a two-quart jar of it, an omer, for future generations . . ." Why? ". . . so they can see the bread that I fed you in the wilderness after I brought you out of Egypt" (THE MESSAGE). It's like a canning jar on the shelf: Remember that harvest? Remember how God rained down bread from heaven? Remember how faithful he is?

Then, just in case they forgot the connection, God instituted three festivals, or feasts, big ceremonies of celebration: the Festival of Unleavened Bread (Remember how God passed over us, and we hurried away with unleavened bread?); the Festival of Harvest (Remember how God grew the seed?); the Festival of Ingathering (Remember how God blessed the work of your hands?). So they could remember—farm, seed, grain, harvest—and trust once again for one more day. Just one more day.

I love the few references in the Scriptures to "shewbread," as the King James Version calls it. What a rich, mysterious term, so dense and almost chewy. David and his hungry men ate it on their way through the tabernacle (1 Samuel 21:6). The Pharisees were still angry about that, hundreds of years later, when Jesus' followers pulled little heads of grain off the stalks in a field and ate them on a Sabbath (Luke 6:1–4).

Shewbread means "bread of the presence." Or even better, presence bread, because each week, priests placed these twelve freshly baked loaves, representing the twelve tribes of Israel, on the table in the sanctuary. "Put the bread of the Presence on this table to be before me at all times," God says (Exodus 25:30).

Before God at all times. The Israelites. Snuggled into the tabernacle, surrounded by shining gold and the glory of God's unfailing presence, those twelve loaves of bread sat before God at all times, always reminding him not to forget his people.

There's a reason bakeries pipe the scent of fresh bread out into the streets. Research in England suggests that the smell of bread baking, or rather, of bread toasting, releases some feel-good hormones that spell contentment and well-being. So having bread that represents God's children always before God's presence, a fragrant aroma, feels homey, like the bread dancing in my bread machine and then served steaming and aromatic to the people I love.

Bread, baked by the priests, set before the God they love, the God who loves them. The God who watches them, sees them, will not forget them, because they sit there, under the mercy seat. A reminder.

A more accurate translation than "bread of the presence" might be "bread of the face." Bread "through which God is seen," says one commentator.[1] Bread that is not only for physical succor but for spiritual nurture as well, because we are before God's face, because through bread we see God's face. Not *in* bread, like a mystical appearance guaranteed to draw crowds and offer healing, but *through* bread, through the provision of bread. See-your-face bread.

I wrestle with this, until I remember a friend's daughter. She was abused as a child and adopted into a loving home. Sometimes her nightmares stalk her like a horror movie, and she screams for her mother to sleep in the second twin bed. The daughter turns toward her mother, staring through the dark for her face, and is comforted.

If my friend shifts her own position and turns over, her child whimpers. "See your face, Momma. See your face."

And in seeing her mother's face, she relaxes. She is safe. Her mother watches over her, so close their fingertips touch.

See your face. Isn't this, ultimately, the cure-all for worry? The Israelites were continually before God's presence. So too are we. Even when we forget, when we don't notice that we are always before God, even when we don't access that presence. Even when people we love aren't watching for God's presence, aren't accessing it, they are no less before God's face. See your face. Because, get this: The Bread of Heaven, Christ, came from heaven, and now "always lives to intercede" for us (Hebrews 7:25) before God. The Bread of Heaven is ever-present before God. See your face.

In fact, the bread motif in the New Testament begins with *Bethlehem,* which means, "city of bread." Christ was born in Bethlehem. The Bread of Heaven came from the city of bread. I want to laugh and also to cheer over this. Nothing like God making a very pointed point.

And then, at the beginning of his earthly ministry, Jesus is propelled into the desert and tempted by the devil. What's one of those primary challenges? "Tell this stone to become bread." And Jesus' response: "It is written: 'Man shall not live on bread alone.'" (See Luke 4:3–4.) This context is intriguing, because the recounting in Luke says Jesus ate nothing for those forty desert days, and when they had ended, he became hungry. But still, he could respond that he lived not only on bread but also feasted on God's presence.

And that's not all. At the Feast of the Passover, Jesus, the Bread of Life, the Bread from heaven, broke the bread, lifted it up, and blessed it. "This is my body, broken, given for you." And later, when Christ returned victorious from the dead, a couple of his disciples hung out with him all day. But it was at the day's end, over the meal, that they recognized Christ in the breaking of the bread. (See Luke 24:29–32.)

This is a lot of bread. Daily Bread. Give us this day, our daily bread. Wherever we find ourselves. However far-flung we might be. Whether we subsist on prison rations or feast at kings' tables, whether we walk through the valley of the shadow of death or have a banquet spread before us, we are God's see-your-face people, always before God's presence.

So, see-your-face bread isn't necessarily a loaf of bread. Not something to load into your shopping cart on the next trip to the grocery store. I consider this, in a year when bread for next month hasn't been a guarantee, though tomorrow seems to be okay. See-your-face bread is any time I stop my whirling and wringing child inside long enough to quit pacing and take stock. I am in God's presence. I breathe this in, a fragrant filling of the lungs of my soul.

If God watches over me, why worry?

God never intended for us to bite off more than one day's worth of food, or life. Gather enough for the day, God says. Daily bread. Don't try to gather more than you need for one day. Don't worry about tomorrow, says Jesus. We've heard it so often it's become trite. But seriously? If we store up, like the hoarded manna, those worries will rot our delight, and our relationships, leaving us writhing with the maggots of fear and discouragement and anxiety.

It's a disgusting image. (I hope you are not having breakfast right now.) But the picture reminds me, when I catapult myself forward into the worries of tomorrow (or next month or next year), that

I am stashing, storing up, a rotting collection. I remember, then: bread of the presence. See your face. Today. I need to just watch, today, because God is watching, and God is present.

Eye contact and focused attention remind us that we are here, that we are okay, that we are loved. When our granddaughter fusses, which is naturally very seldom because she's practically a perfect baby, when she looks into her mother's eyes, when her daddy meets her eyes, she is calmed. Soon her face bursts into a lopsided, my-teeth-are-still-killing-me smile, and her eyes light up. Delight spreads itself over her like the sunrise.

See your face. Who can worry, with eyes like that?

In South Africa, they greet one another with *"Sawubona!"* It means, "I see you!"

The response is *"Yebo!"*

"Yes!"

And God says, today, "I see you!"

And I can say, "Yes!"

Just for today. Not tomorrow, not next month or next year. Today. "I see you!"

"Yes!"

And the Bread of Peace rises in my heart. I inhale. See-your-face bread. My soul expands.

Consider the Wildflowers

There are people in the world so hungry,
that God cannot appear to them except in the form of
bread.[2]

—Mahatma Gandhi

87

Jesus got them all to sit down in groups of fifty or a
hundred—
they looked like a patchwork quilt of wildflowers spread
out on the green grass!
He took the five loaves and two fish, lifted his face to
heaven in prayer, blessed, broke,
and gave the bread to the disciples, and the disciples in
turn gave it to the people.
He did the same with the fish. They all ate their fill.
The disciples gathered twelve baskets of leftovers.
More than five thousand were at the supper.

Mark 6:39–44 THE MESSAGE

1. If Jesus can feed five thousand people with a few rolls and
a couple of fish, with leftovers galore, what application do
you make for your own future, your worry?

2. Try praying the Lord's Prayer slowly at various times when
worry strikes. How does this prayer help you with your worries? What sections reassure you? Which parts are hard to
buy into? In what ways does this prayer reveal God to you?
Yourself to you?

3. When has eye contact with another reassured you? When
have you experienced God's "I see you"? How do you make
eye contact with God? How does that help with your level
of worry?

4. When have you been most aware of God's constancy? What
pulls your focus away from the certainty of God's constant
presence? When?

Votum

Lord,
I remember you
In the breaking of the bread
But I forget you

For much of the rest of my day.
Help me to remember
As the day threatens to break me
That you have broken yourself
Open
For my sake
That I might find my sustenance
In you.
Even as the warm bread is broken apart
And the steamy fragrance fills my senses
May my presence before you
Rise as an offering.
Remember me
Lord Jesus.

Benedictus

Precious One
I see your face
You are ever before me
Always and forever
Because of the fragrant aroma
Of my Son
Broken for you
As near as breath
As close as skin
I see your face
I love your face
I love you.
And so it shall ever be.

6

Wildflower Salsa
The Tool of Movement

Learning the dance of delight . . . even in the anxious seasons of our lives.

I've signed up for salsa dancing," a women's ministry coordinator told me. Celia lived in the nation's breadbasket, not a place I associate with salsa or dancing, unless it's square dancing, but that is likely a stereotype that I should cut from this chapter.

After watching many different shapes and sizes dance in many different styles and venues, even though I personally flunked ballet, I don't think that ability is necessarily related to size or shape, to height or girth. So when my friend said she was taking salsa dancing, I believed her and believed that she would probably be pretty good at it.

Salsa dancing brought Celia to life. Since first meeting her, I thought she should be on the stage with her inordinate gifting for musical theater. But she signed up for salsa dancing not because she thought she had a salsa-dancing shape (about .01 percent of women do, and that's about how many people can actually move their limbs in a salsa-style dance), but because she wanted to get outside of her own Christian life and worries, meet people, and practice. Not dancing, but practice listening and befriending, being a beacon, someone who reflects Christ in this world.

Worry's isolating tendency narrows our focus to our own concerns or to global concerns about which we can do little of any significance. Of course we can do small things with big faith, small things that make a tiny dent in a large problem, but worry isn't one of those tools of impact.

Also, don't people incapacitated by worry likely die sooner because they don't move in constructive ways to help eliminate the destructive energy and caustic effect of stress?* Our immobile and unpracticed hearts become like batteries left too long in a flashlight, corrosive and explosive. The other alternative, I suppose, to worried people dying sooner from lack of constructive movement is that they will live forever nattering away with their worries and annoying everyone in their lives (speaking of corrosive).

My friend Celia's foray into salsa dancing niggled to life a curiosity I've had about the power of movement in stress-filled lives. It probably wasn't the salsa, but King David danced with joy after recovering the ark of the covenant and bringing it back to Jerusalem. In a long parade of celebrating people, King David "was dancing before the Lord with all his might, while he and all Israel were bringing up the ark of the Lord with shouts and the sound of trumpets" (2 Samuel 6:14–15). They'd just defeated the Philistines, were fresh from the stress and worry of war, and then David turned his gaze from battle to worship, dancing with joy, rejoicing in the streets.

---

* This chapter is not an instruction on exercise. Gag. Keep reading. But also, should you decide to take up salsa dancing or any other form of movement to which you are not accustomed, please seek your doctor's advice and approval. This author is not responsible for readers' dancing. ☺

While David danced, his wife Michal watched from the window as the king humbled himself in dance, her face tight with fury and embarrassment. David would need those feel-good endorphins from the worship and the festive dance when he returned home.

Dancing isn't one of my fortes, but movement as a tool to combat worry doesn't require skill—just mobility, and one step at a time.

I flunked ballet as a six-year-old (my mother tells me I didn't flunk, I withdrew). A lifetime later, it's etched into my mind like a carving: the awkward self-centered focus of the time and my gawky, skinny, plaintive form and face, as well as the pale pink leotard, which made me look like I needed a transfusion, a slower metabolism, and high-calorie, weight-gaining supplements. The locker room scent of the studio where some danced, and where I lunged and stumbled about, returns to me in a full-sensory package of mortification. It seemed that coordination of movement beyond bike riding and normal childhood play had been withheld from me and my share distributed to, say, the cute twins across the street, who looked adorable in their leotards and little ballet shoes. They were short and strong and compact and had beautiful dancers' feet, with toes that pointed perfectly.

This plaguing sense of awkwardness trailed me to my two dates in high school, sadly, homecoming and prom, and the absolute death-wish I had around about that time, basically from the moment my date arrived until he dropped me back at home. (No, wait, now I remember that the misery extended for days afterward, when friends related in glowing details the romance and beauty of their evenings.) My dates were fine, upstanding young men, but I always thought I was their pity date, and the actual dance itself was beyond embarrassing. For me, at least. The scene from *It's a Wonderful Life,* where the gym floor splits apart and Jimmy

Stewart, Donna Reed, and the other dancers fall into the swimming pool would have been welcome during those over-hyped and ghastly milestones.

No woman wants to attend a dance with a date and have it be less than a wonderful evening—but she also wants others to think she looks good. In my surveys of women, it turns out that a lot of us worry about what other people think of us. Movement is no exception. What relief we'd experience if we realized the truth of Eleanor Roosevelt's words: "You wouldn't worry so much about what others think of you if you realized how seldom they do."

But we don't realize that. I toddled off to college with my worry lens focused on boyfriends and the next test, the drama in the dorms, and the occasional school dance, which I attended with fear, and learned in some rather embarrassing ways to move in rhythm. There I met the first exhilaration of movement, grateful those dances were held in darkened lobbies of dorms.

I managed not to worry about the distant future too much, which is a bit shortsighted since (a) worry helps so much and (b) the future was sliding awfully close when graduation neared. Those years would turn into the last worry-free era of my life. I recognize now that the lack of worry was due to the essential knowledge that my parents were providing for me.

Once on my own, life became serious. No more ridiculous dancing. Ever. Lots more Serious Call to a Devout and Holy Life.

Perhaps I'd have made the transition more smoothly had I been more emotionally and spiritually mature and realized that I could simply shift parental protection—if I'd deliberately acknowledged my God in heaven, whose protection is far more life-sustaining and life-giving and broad than the caring protection my parents could offer.

But worry was, and still is, perhaps, a great untalked-of issue. It is still spiritualized (if we aren't worrying, then maybe we don't care), and many still believe that if we are "burdened" about something then we are godly.

So I thought I was doing myself a favor by worrying? That's a stretch. But worry's constant distraction depleted my energies. I'd always been active (read: busy), but only in brief spurts of deliberate exercise. Any rounds of exercise enthusiasm lasted a few weeks at best. Racquetball in college. A brief stint at newlywed jogging, until I collapsed on a sidewalk in pain and had to lie there until I could crawl back to our apartment. After that, I ran after children and ran into church meetings and raised my blood pressure and cholesterol levels but not my metabolism. And worry, constant worry, showing up as irritability, fear, and a paper-thin emotional fragility, stalked me.

Doctors have said for years, "Even if you don't have a dog, walk your dog." Because walking, movement, helps both body and soul. Exercise sends feel-good endorphins throughout our bodies, going to work on anxiety. Then, sometime in the last few years, after literal physical chest pain from so much worry, I read that the rote movement of walking boosts creativity levels.

So body, soul, creativity: Movement helps all three. I began to exercise, finding some ancient videos (undoubtedly free) like *Sweating to the Oldies* and also Paula Abdul in her 1990s workout wear. The irony that these are dance routines is not lost on me: ironic because I can't dance. Ironic because I am uncoordinated. It also isn't lost on me that the elevation of my heart rate made me feel better in just about every way. Physically, emotionally, relationally, and work-wise. Uncoordinated or not, I was more alive because of the movement.

Billy Blanks tutored me in DVD Tae Bo. Who knew I could kick and punch and develop an actual core? Billy traveled with me to all my engagements, even to the Philippines, and again, the power of movement won over the stress and worry of a hectic but sometimes sedentary life.

Movement helps our hearts. Adds endorphins to our cache of hormones. It increases our joy baseline, though I haven't seen that in research, just lived that reality. Movement converts worry to positive energy. There is no way around that.

Otherwise, worry is like having a sieve in the bottom of my soul, so that anything I put in just pours straight through. I retain none of the nutritional value of the intake. But movement somehow seals those holes, at least temporarily, and thus the water level in both soul and psyche rises.

Movement heals. Recently, in physical therapy for a heel injury, I mentioned that I'd stayed off my feet at the advice of a coach until I could see a doctor. The physical therapist, a brilliant young woman from Romania, disagreed, saying that movement heals, increasing blood flow and bringing healing oxygen to the wounded area.

Oxygen. Air. And the word for breath in Hebrew? *Ruach*. Breath, life, life force, God-breathed.

A woman struggling with major depression wrote, telling me that when she started getting serious about working out at the gym, her worry level lessened. Exercise, both cardio and weight-lifting, boosted her metabolism, her energy, and her mood. She had fewer worried and dark depressive days if she moved.

Maybe "Move it or lose it" is a good slogan for worriers; move it or lose our cool, our temper, relationships, health, friends, a happy home . . . and our energy. Don't the Scriptures tell us, "Walk by faith" (2 Corinthians 5:7 ESV)? They don't say, "Sit by faith," "Wring your hands by faith," or "Pace by faith."

Rather, walk by faith. Run the race. Move. Put feet to your worries and then watch them fall behind you on the dance floor, or the sidewalk, or the track. Walk. Run. Move. Dance. Live.

After a number of years of sporadic exercise (Billy and I broke off our relationship because I developed Tae-Bo elbows), I learned that our health insurance program offered incentives for using a pedometer. I could get paid for taking steps.

This device keeps me moving and fooled me into believing it's not actually exercise or work. No one is more surprised than I: In a recent contest, I ranked in the top twenty in our area, and the top 200 in the nation. *Moi*, Miss Uncoordinated, Miss I Hate Exercise, Miss Last Person Chosen on the Playground. Even in a period of high stress, travel, deadlines, and worries, I aim for 12,000 steps per day. Some of those are actual walking, steps to and fro, up and down airport corridors, to the mailbox and grocery store. But at least a third I log using Cardio Dance DVDs (free, of course, from the library, need you ask?). Exercise for the sake of exercise still reduces me to absolute anxiety and dismay, but I look forward to these little cardio dance sessions in the privacy of my own home or travel accommodations.

I'm learning. I'm not as uncoordinated as I believed—maybe no one is, if we can just be kind and patient with ourselves. It's not an audition, after all, unless we're auditioning for life. Which might be the case. We can learn movement, we can train our bodies to respond and work. The combination of music and movement works in a way nothing else does for me. And for those forty minutes (if you'd told me ten years ago that forty minutes of my day would be given willingly to cardio, I'd have kicked and screamed and left home) I am free of worry, free in a way that continues for hours. Even when plowing back to my desk and my writing, even when rushing out the door at four in the morning for a flight, if I've exercised, my worry lessens and my mood elevates.

I feel like Mme. Marie Curie, like I've discovered the cure for some dread disease.

Maybe that's true.

One Sunday when my husband headed into a new church to facilitate worship, a man greeted him at the door from a wheelchair, his seat for a number of years. They spoke briefly prior to the service, but he needed to greet and Rich needed to set up equipment. Later, Rich invited some of the congregation up to help lead the closing song, "Lord of the Dance."

The man in the wheelchair rolled right up that center aisle and took a place in front.

And he danced.

In church.

In a wheelchair.

Dance. Worship. Joy. On wheels.

My husband and I drove through a nearby small town with our son in the back seat. At twenty-two, he's full of instant wit, making me wish I had a video camera constantly shooting footage and wonder why he doesn't have his own show.

The town's growing population boasted a new Zumba business. "I'm gonna take me a Zumba class there," I said, pointing at the tiny wedge-shaped building.

The guys were off. Both assumed foreign accents and Josh spouted a hundred sentences, a riff that drove us all the way home, Zumba in each phrase. Zumbanité! Zumbaté! Zumbona! Zumbini (a hat one wears whilst Zumbaing, he defined). The two of them had me leaning against the car door in hysterics.

The snow, meanwhile, had piled up in our driveway, so we sprang from the car for shovels before driving in. Up and down the long asphalt, Josh skated and shoveled, all the while shouting Zumba words, all sounding like "Charge!"

The dark moonless night, snow-dancing down the fresh black swath of exposed driveway as Josh sluiced through the night, calling out, "Zum-baaaaah!" Even now, my chest expands with laughter.

You can't laugh and worry, move and worry, shovel and worry, Zumba and worry, simultaneously. And if you don't have your own Zumboni, grab a shovel. Just ask my son, the ambassador for Zumbabwe.

People clapped, perspiration dripped, feet moved expertly in this native dance of the Philippines. Young, lean, muscular bodies performed feats impossible for normal mortals. As the dance progressed, the pace increased, displaying the dancers' grace and fleet-footedness. Then the invitation sounded, "Who wants to learn the *Tinikling*?"

With high humidity, high temperatures, sleep deprivation, intense ministry, and a fourteen-hour time difference—not to mention general lack of dance ability on my part—my learning a sweaty, complicated, intense jumping dance was beyond anything I could imagine, or desire. I avoided eye contact with everyone on the piazza.

But my new friends raised a chorus: "Jane! Jane wants to learn the Tinikling!"

Oh dear. My heart plummeted and, impossibly, even more sweat poured out of my pores. I was too empty to learn, too distracted and dehydrated, too tired. Too embarrassed. Terrified.

But a ridiculously fit dancer pulled me to my feet, dragging me to the patio-turned-dance-floor. This was one of my worst nightmares: uncoordination in public places.

Two long poles rested parallel on the ground, with just enough room between them for our feet. Our job was to jump over these poles in unison. Jumping wouldn't be a problem if the poles were stationary, but no. Young men squatted at either end, grasping the poles with both hands, and smacked them together, then banged them into the floor, together again, then down. But not in a 1-2-3-4 rhythm or pattern, at least not that my worry-filled brain could discern, and always faster.

I envisioned bruised—or broken!—ankles and a battered self-esteem. The latter is less critical than the former: It is hard to travel with banged-up ankles damaged from being slammed between bamboo poles. But my partner allowed no time for weighing the plan's demerits. He clasped my hands and the poles started to smack together. I leapt out of the way.

When I stared at his feet, sometimes I could command my own to follow, always just a second late. Then I started thinking and worrying. The sticks stopped and clanked to the ground. Thankfully.

My partner said, "Miss Jane, just look into my eyes. Then you can dance the Tinikling."

This seemed ridiculous and unlikely. Not to mention unsafe. How do you trust your feet if you can't see them? But his grip reminded me that I was in the hands of an expert. Maybe he knew what he was talking about.

So I watched his eyes. I'd like to be able to write about how wonderful the next moments were, that my next gig would be on *Dancing With the Stars*. Or not. For a few measures, I looked into his eyes and lost my self-consciousness. For fleeting seconds we danced the Tinikling. For the rest of it, I stumbled and held on and dragged my gaze back to my partner's. But we laughed a great deal (at my expense, but that's still a good joke) and my friends cheered and patted me on the back when the ordeal—I mean, experience—ended.

I swiped at my brow, willing my heart to calm. Reentering my life, with its stumbling dance of faith, I try to start each day with Scripture, with prayer, but find my gaze wrenched away to something needing fixing in home, or office, or life, or relationships, or work. I look at my calendar and worries intensify: There is either too much, or too little, on the pages before me. I glance at my list of to-dos and groan at the impossibility of it all.

Then I hear, "Watch my eyes, Miss Jane. Then you can dance."

Don't the Scriptures affirm, "Let us fix our eyes on *Jesus* . . ." (Hebrews 12:2 NIV1984)? Fix our eyes. To see, notice, perceive. To watch. And then, in verse 3: "Consider him." To think carefully about. This seeing, this considering, this watching Jesus' eyes, is a deliberate lifting of our gaze. A choice.

My list is too long, my resources too short; worries render me klutzy spiritually and in relationship with people I love. Today, I stop with the lists and fears. I think carefully about Jesus, who said, "With you it's impossible. With me, all things are possible" (see Matthew 19:26). I look around, and see, notice, perceive that all we have is from Christ's hand, both literally and spiritually.

And my heart leaps, evading the slamming poles of worry and fear and exhaustion. My soul dances a thank-you jig.[1]

Consider the Wildflowers

> If these Christians want me to believe in their god,
> they'll have to sing better songs,
> they'll have to look more like people who have been saved,
> they'll have to wear on their countenance the joy of the
>   beatitudes.
> I could only believe in a god who dances.[2]
>
> —Friedrich Nietzsche, 1844–1900

Oh, visit the earth, ask her to join the dance!
Deck her out in spring showers, fill the God-River with liv-
    ing water.
Paint the wheat fields golden.
Creation was made for this! Drench the plowed fields, soak
    the dirt clods
With rainfall as harrow and rake bring her to blossom and
    fruit.
Snow-crown the peaks with splendor, scatter rose petals
    down your paths,

All through the wild meadows, rose petals.
Set the hills to dancing,
Dress the canyon walls with live sheep, a drape of flax
across the valleys.
Let them shout, and shout, and shout!
Oh, oh, let them sing!

Psalm 65:9–13 THE MESSAGE

1. Physical movement keeps our body systems moving, and clearly, this is important for health. But what about spiritual movement? In what ways does your physical movement (or lack of) parallel your spiritual movement? What connection do you see between your liveliness physically, emotionally, and spiritually?

2. Like Michal berated her husband, King David, for dancing in a way *she* considered inappropriate, what messages about movement have you heard (or interpreted) throughout your life? For instance, did people tell you to settle down, or not make a scene? Or slow down? Stop jiggling? Or the opposite: Get up, get going, get off your rear, you are lazy. How have they impacted you, your sense of self and coordination, and/ or your worry levels?

3. Movement leads to improvement—creatively, physically, spiritually, even relationally. How would this relate to worry? And if you took yourself less seriously, and your life more seriously, what would change for you in terms of spiritual and physical movement?

4. When I first started trying to move more, I was embarrassed even when I was alone! But I've been surprised to realize that I'm not as uncoordinated as I always felt. It took a while before it felt remotely fun, however. But my obsessional worries lessened almost immediately and the reprieve lasted for hours. How could you experiment with the movement-worry connection?

Votum

Oh Lord.
More guilt.
Now I need to move more?
I can barely keep up with my brain
And my life
Now.
Help me to move toward you
In all ways
That I might become more limber
Of soul
And less rigid with worry.
Increase in me
Guide my steps
Be my partner
In this dance
That is life.

Benedictus

Oh, honey!
I just want to see your joy
I want to see your eyes
And the light in them
Because we are together
And I am your dance partner
You will never be a wallflower
Because you are mine.
So come
Dance with me
Laugh with me
And together we will evade
The clanging poles
Of worry.
May I
Have
This dance?

7

Watered by Tears
The Tool of Tears

*Tears teach us and help us to live beyond worry.
Learning to wait with the tears until God waters the
parched soil of our souls. Delight waits for us, in the
tears.*

Worry complicates our lives—and health—in ways we can't imagine. One of the most surprising tools in the arsenal of worry-combat is tears. Tears, those saltwater droplets that spill at the most inopportune times. The smidgens of moisture that destroy our eyeliner so that we try to fan away the damp with our hands. (This works really well; try it sometime and see how clever you look). We ignore them, look at the ceiling in hopes of absorbing them. We blink, pretend to have allergies. We dam them up, putting a plug in one of the most ingenious recovery weapons God has devised.

Tears. Tears will teach us about worry. They will teach us about ourselves, about our hearts, about our past and our future, about our hopes and our hurts. They will teach us about others. And used with integrity, these little tools help us to heal, redirecting our focus away from our multilayered worries, to God.

Deep healing began for Melissa (not her real name) when her son toddled into her, smacking her chin with his forehead. At the child's impact, Melissa's head jerked back, setting off a chain reaction in her body. Throughout the day, her head continued to snap back and forth. The involuntary movement surprised her, but she had a full house, a schedule, kids to tend, a husband coming home soon. She figured, "This will pass."

It did not pass. In fact, her body seized the opportunity to begin a lockdown—a lockdown that would first devastate her and her family but eventually lead her toward wholeness. She lost her strength. Then her legs stopped working, confining her to a wheelchair. By now, the worry bells tolled constantly for Melissa and her husband. They sought round after round of medical advice. Her diagnosis shifted with each specialist. Melissa lived with the sentence of Muscular Sclerosis. Or maybe, doctors thought, Muscular Dystrophy. Or maybe . . .

Before long, paralysis imprisoned her. She could barely hold her children. But when she started losing her eyesight, her desperation peaked. Nearly bankrupt, they splurged on one more specialist, who examined the piles of medical records while the young couple waited, hearts nearly as paralyzed as her legs. Steeped in fear, Melissa could hardly imagine any return to normalcy. In her present incapacitated state, it would just be nice to see again. See her husband, her children, the beauty outside. See anything. But after so many disappointments and so much despair, she refused to hope.

The doctor finished studying the records and looked up. "I don't believe you have any of these other diagnoses," he said, tapping the stack of documents. "You have what is known as conversion disorder."[1]

Our bodies, brilliantly designed, will convert ungrieved and unfelt emotions into bodily symptoms, including paralysis, loss of speech, and impaired vision, if we don't take care of those emotions. Melissa, like many women, came to Christ and believed that her past was indeed behind her. Don't the Scriptures affirm, "See, I am doing a new thing!" (Isaiah 43:19 NIV1984) and "The old has gone, the new has come!" (2 Corinthians 5:17 NIV1984)?

Yes. And no. Because Jesus isn't magic, and healing often requires deliberate effort on our part. Under doctor's orders, Melissa started counseling. As she grieved, weeping over a painful and abusive past, feeling returned. To her heart, yes. But also to her body. She regained her sight. She left her wheelchair at a resale shop. She gathered her family into her arms. Now, she does the work necessary to live freely each day, to grieve as needed so no stockpile builds on the inside of her soul.

What a phenomenon. These tiny drops that pool or drip or puddle lead to healing, in multiple ways. When we weep with emotions like grief, anger, or pain, the tears contain prolactin, a hormone that stimulates the release of breast milk. Another component of tears is adrenocorticotropic, a stress-produced hormone.[2] So scientifically speaking, not just emotionally or intuitively on my part, tears enable us to expel stress-related hormones. They are part of God's detox system. Tears literally make us feel better.

Maybe this is why people say, "I feel better after a good cry."

But weeping isn't accepted in many circles, cultures, and church communities. Women are taught not to cry because tears are manipulative, or a sign of weakness. Or they're unladylike. (This one makes me laugh.) We're supposed to just get over it, whatever *it* is. Tears, some women learn early on, are a pity party and that belief sends them on a guilt trip. And the cycle begins again.

In order to tap into the keg of tears we probably tote around, and to benefit from that reservoir, begin by noticing some of those cryptic orders. Haven't we all heard some variation of these?

Dry up. Buck up.

Don't cry . . . it'll be okay. (Pat pat pat on the back.)

Stop crying or I'll give you something to cry about.

You think you've got it bad?

Cry baby.

We hear these often enough and sometimes we just stop crying. Once a woman mentioned she hadn't cried in years. What, I asked, was happening when you stopped crying? What messages about tears have you heard in your lifetime, and from whom?

Maybe we need to reexamine those messages and separate the lies from the truth. Tears are inconvenient, messy, and leave us (and others) uncomfortable and helpless to fix them. All true. *Runny black mascara streaks look ghastly, dahling.* But since when is healing convenient or classy? Or clean? Since when are natural body processes comfortable? Tears are excretions, just like sweat, urine, exhaled breath.

Not engaging with tears keeps us safe. So we think. But when did we begin to believe that staying safe was the best way to live? Safety does not equate to living. It means we choose to simply get by with a minimum of fuss and attention, and even less risk. Until our body takes over, like it did for Melissa, and demands the attention deserved this vessel that must carry us around for the rest of our life. Unshed tears equal unfelt grief or pain and can lead to physical, relational, and spiritual difficulty.

If we allow the tears space to express themselves, they will help us heal, move us forward, back into life. Tears can help us notice and relinquish our worry about what others think of us, what God thinks of us, what we think of ourselves. Tears can teach us. Our souls are smart and our God is smart. We are designed to shed tears, whether to flush out irritants in our eyes, or as a response to acrid fumes like onions or tear gas or

Cajun seasoning . . . or as a response to life's joys and delights and worries and regrets.

Such power in tears, such miracle in weeping.

This mysterious solution of tears can't just be broken down into chemical compounds. Tears signal us

That we are alive.

That a work is waiting to be done.

That life and hope and healing are at hand.

That heaven knocks at the door.

So we notice where the tears appear: the baby snow boots at the door, abandoned by a visiting child, long gone. The surprising scent of lilacs, blowing on the breeze like wanton perfume. Giggles in church from a pew of teenagers. The hymn last week. The clack of a hockey stick on ice. The funeral of someone we barely know. The beauty of the ocean, tiny footprints following me in the sand and pressed into my soul. What messages these damp messengers speak.

Poignant memories do not always evoke, or invoke, tears. Once the neighbors' violent arguments set me pacing in our newlywed apartment, and I had to sit outside on the stoop until the fear and the tears subsided.

Once I saw the ugly cruelty of a dad angry with his son outside a hardware store. He forced the boy to bend at the waist and put his bare hands into a snowbank for an extended time. The child tried to hold back tears, but I was not so brave. I'd never seen that kind of abuse, and it opened my heart to a panorama of wounded children, a world full of refugees who want only to escape the tyranny of pain in their past.

Tears whisper of the tiptoe presence of God, the kind attention of the Holy Spirit. Perhaps tears are a love song from God, inviting us into sanctuary, where we rest and heal and notice and see. And live. The gentlest of invitations to explore without shame, to cleanse bacteria and infection from the eyes of our soul.

We wait with our tears, stay with them like a mother with a brokenhearted child, knowing the tears are both an invitation from God to us, and from us to God.

Tears are like a Rototiller; you never know what might turn up. What if we unearth stumps of anger, roots of unforgiveness, fieldstones of shame or regret? None of these discoveries will kill us—exposed to the air and the sunlight and the Son of Light, these uprooted finds begin to heal, one at a time, with deliberate kindness and attention. Yours, and perhaps some other trusted soul, for it isn't always good or healthy to weep alone, to uproot pain in isolation. And please know that excessive tears might indicate the need for professional/medical help. There is no shame in needing someone skilled to wade through the waters of pain with us.

In the tilling, we might also churn up worry, which seems connected to all the other possibilities. Worry about what might happen if we cry now—maybe we will never stop, our tears will turn to an endless gushing, an Old Faithful geyser of weeping. Worry about what others will think of us. Worry that nothing will change. Or that everything will change, and where would that leave us? Once again, in unfamiliar terrain.

And worry, of course, about an endless litany of events and people beyond our tenuous (or even mythical) realm of control.

Once, a prison-release program visited our adult Sunday school class. The presenters, former prisoners, spoke with passion and tears about their journeys.

I, in my Sunday school chair and my shut-down heart's self-righteousness, tuned them out entirely. Later I told my husband, "He needed more healing before he started speaking."

This, from my folding metal judgment seat, my push-through, gut-it-out, tears-are-a-luxury-you-can't-afford self. My "if Jesus heals you, there's no place for tears" faulty theology. I feel sad, remembering that now. Because now I know that tears are not a luxury. They are essential, progressive, and offer the possibility of becoming whole. Or at least closer to whole.

In fairness, I hadn't always seen tears used in a positive or healing manner. They'd seemed manipulative in my experience of other women's weeping. They'd too often felt destructive and untrustworthy, conjured up for dramatic or hurtful impact.

And also in journalistic fairness, tears hadn't worked for me. They hadn't helped me get my way, hadn't helped change other people, hadn't strengthened any cause for which I felt passion. I didn't feel better after crying, just embarrassed and self-indulgent. Like I'd wasted my energy.

I slid into the restaurant booth across from my friend. "How are you, really, Jane?" she asked. She referred to an ongoing saga, a persistent and chronic worry, in our family. She prayed—still prays—for us daily.

After a deep breath, I said, "I'm on the tears-every-day diet." I swiped at my eyes and smiled a real smile. "But I think it's keeping me alive."

It's true. Because my tears connected me to my worry, and worry connected me to my tears, and both connected me to my soul and to the God of my soul and indeed the God of the universe. That vital tethering saved my life.

Morning after morning, I encountered God's faithfulness, God's new mercies, through the Scriptures, through deep reading. Through tears. I wrote in my journal one dawn, "Feeling sad, tired, lonely, like a blown-out Easter egg. Very fragile. My heart is trying to tell me something, and the only language it has right now is tears."

Without tears, my heart would have burst, imploded from worry without a safety valve. It's possible that I would now be a pile of bones in a box underground. Or that my soul would have turned into a scrap of rawhide, dried and withered. The great chew toy of worry.

A women's ministry director, we'll call her Kathy, welcomed me into the church. We chatted while I set up and she gathered materials and leaders and other people. Her father died just weeks before, and even as she spoke, her eyes flooded with tears. She turned away from the other women for privacy.

"I don't want to cry when I lead next week," she said.

I wondered about that. "Don't you think women need to see you cry? It gives them permission to feel their own pain, and to shed their own tears."

Our tears, as women in leadership, women who are friends, daughters, wives, or mothers, or all of the above, invite other women to weep as well. Our humanity allows them to be human, to set aside their Bible study leader/Good Christian Woman mask. Like a baby in a nursery, hearing another infant wail sets off her own crying jag. Soon the nursery erupts in crying babies. Yes, a crazy cacophony, but also a well-orchestrated reminder that we all have wounds and worries that need to heal.

And together, in community, we begin to heal.

Physiologically speaking, without tears, our eyes would dry out and we would eventually lose our sight. And isn't it true spiritually and emotionally as well? Paul said, "I pray that the eyes of your heart may be enlightened" (Ephesians 1:18), and when we can weep, our hearts begin to see again.

Our worries might not evaporate with our tears—but tears create space for faith. Faith. The opposite of worry.

And just to counteract the inevitable *tsk-tsking* we might experience if we spout tears, consider the Scriptures that invite us to weep, to cry, to mourn, and grieve. Might as well add these to our arsenal of tools, because it sounds to me as if God not only created tears, he endorses them.

> Yet the Lord longs to be gracious to you; therefore he will rise up to show you compassion. For the Lord is a God of justice. Blessed are all who wait for him! People of Zion, who live in Jerusalem, you will weep no more. How gracious he will be when you cry for help! As soon as he hears, he will answer you.
>
> Isaiah 30:18–19

Romans 12:15–16 says, "Rejoice with those who rejoice; mourn with those who mourn. Live in harmony with one another." This injunction sets off a wordless cantata of praise within me: praise that as we rejoice with one another, regardless of how much better another's fortune than ours; as we weep with one another, regardless of whose situation is more dire, whose worries more intense; as we follow these basic rules of community grace, we begin to live in harmony with one another. Weep with those who weep.

Isn't this why the Israelites had professional mourners, people who started the nursery of tears, the wails of communal weeping? Isn't this why the psalmist tells us, "Record my misery; list my tears on your scroll—are they not in your record?" (56:8). (The original language may mean, "Record my misery; put my tears in your wine-skin.") A wineskin full of our tears. There's a reason the Wailing Wall is one of the most popular sites in Israel. Community grief is not only accessible, it is acceptable, respectable, and expected.

And wasn't that how Jesus, who wept when Lazarus died (John 11:35), and wept for Jerusalem, and wept over God's will that dreadful night in the garden of Gethsemane, said people would recognize us as his followers—by our love for one another?

Tears—weeping—grieving with one another, are means of establishing both community and acceptance, as well as a witness to the world.

"My!" people will say. "See how they love one another."

So we weep with those who weep, and the world watches and wants to join the celebration. To be loved like that is part of everyone's deepest longing. (And a great eradicator of worry.)

And while we're in for the penny, we might as well go in for the pound. We might as well hold on for the final gift. Jesus, in the great conversion effect—maybe it's conversion order instead of conversion disorder!—of tears, said, "Blessed are you who weep now, for you will laugh" (Luke 6:21). Imagine that. You will laugh, he says! Echoes of Jeremiah, "I'll convert their weeping into laughter, lavishing comfort, invading their grief with joy" (31:13 THE MESSAGE). Laughing, the catharsis of weeping. Rejoicing comes in the morning.[3]

And we, like women in the field, sow our worries in tears and reap from the furrows the seeds of delight, tiding us over until one day God will rip off our black mourning bands and deck us with wildflowers (Psalm 30:11–12 THE MESSAGE). A lei of beauty to replace our tears. As Revelation 21:4 exults, God will personally wipe away every tear from our eyes, and there will be no more death or mourning or crying or pain.

And no more worry. If we start now, we'll be ready for heaven. And maybe even ready for tomorrow.

Tears press.

God knocks.

Say yes.

Hello healing.

Goodbye worry.

·❀· Consider the Wildflowers ·❀·

You never know what may cause them. The sight of the Atlantic Ocean can do it, or a piece of music, or a face you've never seen before. A pair of somebody's old shoes can do it. Almost any movie made before the great sadness that came over the world after the Second World War. . . . You can never be sure. But of this you can be sure. Whenever you find tears in your eyes, especially unexpected tears, it is well to pay the closest attention.

They are not only telling you something about the secret of who you are, but more often than not God is speaking to you through them of the mystery of where you have come from and is summoning you to where, if your soul is to be saved, you should go to next.[4]

—Frederick Buechner, *Listening to Your Life*

> Then young women will dance and be glad,
>   young men and old as well.
> I will turn their mourning into gladness;
>   I will give them comfort and joy instead of sorrow.
>
> Jeremiah 31:13

1. Sometimes we overreact to others because we haven't adequately acknowledged or felt our own feelings. Sometimes our tears for another tap into our own unattended worries and grief. When have you experienced this?

2. What messages did you receive about tears growing up? How about as an adult? How has that impacted you? In what ways might this affect your worrying?

3. Isaiah 30:18–19 tells us to cry out to God, and then, "As soon as he hears, he will answer you." When do you feel like God hears your tears? When does it seem like God is taking forever to answer, or has maybe turned a deaf ear? What do you do in those times?

4. What do you learn about yourself through tears? About your relationships with others, with God?

Votum

Dear God
They say you store

My tears
In a bottle
But I feel invisible to you
With all my worries
Like perhaps you have a deaf ear
A tear-deaf heart.
Could you show me that you hear?
My bed is wet with my tears
So if you could wring me out
And ring me up
And answer my call.
I need you.

Benedictus

Child, child,
Of course I hear you
And the heavens weep
With my tears for you
I am the God of compassion
And I wait for you to call to me.
I hear you
I am on the way
I have sent my Son
To bear your sorrows
So keep calling
I am answering
And the Comforter comes.
Bring me your burdens
Your worries
And see what flowers
Grow
From the furrows
Of pain.

8

The Silent Walk
The Tool of Empathy

Acknowledging the worrisome commonalities of our journey, and the courage it costs to walk in this world. A little pain goes a long, long way, but we can walk it away.

Laughter bounced from the wooden ceiling, draped over the crossbeams, warmed the gathering room of our women's retreat. These ladies loved each other, had been friends for years in many cases. The rapport was lovely and bright. Working with our theme of transitions, of powerful choices in powerless places, the coordinators capitalized on the idea of a journey. One of the ice breakers (I know, I loathe them too, but especially dislike having to come up with them) they called "The Silent Walk."

All of us lined up on one side of the room, against a wall. The damaged hardwood floor lay before us, its history carved into the scuffs and dents and scratches of its planks. A moderator stood at one end of the room. When we could say yes to one of the statements she called out, she instructed us to walk across the room to the opposite wall. As we crossed the floor and then turned and stood, separated from the rest of the crowd, we noticed one another. Then we returned to the safe anonymity of the gang and awaited the next call.

In this empathy-building exercise, we were to cross the room if the statement reflected our own situation or that of someone we loved. Some of the statements were silly, like, "Walk across the room if you have dyed your hair." "If you have on jeans." Or "underwear." For the most part, the statements were fairly non-threatening and innocuous (unless you were going commando that day, having forgotten to pack a change of undies). Some statements were almost universal: "Walk across the room if you or someone you love is ill." Who doesn't know someone who is ill?

But then the circumstances changed, deepened. "Walk across the room if you or someone you love needs a different job." Or is unemployed. Or has suffered a miscarriage. As the scenarios became increasingly weighty, my heart, too, gained weight—the weight of others' sorrow, the heft of pain, of brokenness, of disappointment.

Walk across the room if . . . you or someone you love has been arrested, or is in jail, or is gay, or is in a broken marriage, or has a prodigal child, or is going through a divorce, or has a house going into foreclosure, or has an addiction, or. . . . As we stepped out onto that scarred floor, bearing and baring our own scars and heartbreak, the mood changed from one of jovial laughter to one of respect and empathy. A holy hush settled over us like a mist at dawn. Though no one spoke, the body language of broken dreams and sorrow telegraphed a message to all of us. Tears sprang to our eyes, our lips tightened or turned down; we swallowed as we glanced at our comrades.

To hazard a guess, I would say that all of us crossed that room, acknowledging the truth of statements we perhaps had never before admitted to a wider audience than family or best friend, or a small group of confidantes. And though details were not shared—no one was forced to talk about the job loss or prodigal child or anything at all in large- or small-group time—any sense of separation seemed to disintegrate. Any possibility of judgment likewise disappeared, like gasoline evaporating into the air. The load women carried moved me, the sheer courage required day after day to take up their mantle and walk forward into their lives.

And none of us, having been on the other side of the room, could possibly feel alone in our troubles and our worries.

When troubles and worries do their worst, they separate us from our own souls and our God. They isolate us from people who love us, who understand, who could walk alongside us on our toiling way. We lose our capacity to feel another's pain, because our own worries sheathe us like armor.

But even more, this separation, this dearth of empathy, not only dehumanizes us, but dehumanizes others in their painful places and bewildering circumstances, their worry-filled lives that rattle like a beggar's cup, looking for the spare change of hope.

Empathy becomes the currency that goes beyond allaying our own anxiety and fear. With the tool of empathy, we pull back the camera to a broader focal point, expanding beyond our own worries to others' lives and burdens.

Studies have shown that given the theoretical option of exchanging our unique package of problems and worries for another's set, most people say, "I'll take my own, thank you. I don't see how they keep going." The tool of empathy isn't the same as comparing our miseries and deciding others have it worse or even far worse, so we should buck up. It is less about that perspective—although that renders our issues easier to bear than the wagonload of pain others pull.

Rather, empathy, as Webster puts it, is "The capacity for participation in another's feelings or ideas."[1] Addiction psychiatrist David Sack, MD, says, "In its broadest sense, empathy is central to what it means to be fully human. It allows us to tune in to how someone else is feeling and gives us insights into the thoughts, emotions and behaviors of other people."[2] Isn't this what Romans 12:15 (NLT) tells us to do, "Weep with those who weep"?

Jeremiah's empathy for his people bleeds through Lamentations: "My eyes fail from weeping, I am in torment within; my heart is poured out on the ground because my people are destroyed, because children and infants faint in the streets of the city" (Lamentations 2:11).

This spins 'round in my brain for a bit. I have trouble stopping the pinwheel and paying attention. Because somewhere, over this past decade of too much work and worry, too little sleep and refilling, that section of my soul has hardened over, like the fontanel on a baby's soft, fuzzy scalp fusing together too soon. Worry has reduced me to being less than fully human. While I am aware of others' pain and feelings, actually entering into them—literally feeling the pain, suffering with them, which is the definition and root of the word *compassion*—seems more than I can bear. I confess I feel more like a pothole than a deep well. I'm afraid that my worrying has made me shallow.

This isn't always true across the board—it hasn't stopped me from loving others, from caring for them. Usually I am still nice to people en route. But the more I traveled, the more stories I heard, the more nightmares I had. Once during a retreat in the mountain ranges out west, women waited in line to talk with me. And each woman had a story worse than the woman before her. Stories of sexual abuse as children, of abusive husbands; stories of addiction, fear, illness, depression, eating disorders.

I returned to my room with literal pain in my heart and prayed throughout the night. When I finally slept, I dreamt about these women and their difficulties, awakening with a dark cloud surrounding my soul.

That morning, my husband, who had accompanied me to the conference, said, "You can't carry their pain. You have to give it to God, or others' pain will destroy you."

The answer wasn't, isn't, to stop caring. The answer is to continue to feel, and to carry those feelings to God. Then, freed up of our burdens, we reenter the fray armed with God's love. God's empathy.

We know this. This is such a basic rule for emotional health.

Reading about empathy, I find an interesting—convicting—correlation between addiction and empathy, or rather the lack of empathy. This shouldn't surprise me, because it makes sense, but still, I am surprised. Some 12-Step groups have a sign that says, simply, *We care*. This is a statement of current activity and safety and agenda: We care in this place. Around this table, we care for one another. We care for, and take care of, ourselves, rather than expecting others to do so, or hoping for something magical to happen to erase our problems and dysfunction.

But *We care* is also an affirmation, a reminder that as an addict heals, the critical component of empathy must also return, or healing and recovery will not only be hindered, they will be aborted. Caring is both critical to, and a sign of, recovery.

In addictive living, the capacity to care is reduced to a single, myopic focus: self. The addict begins to care about only herself, only her needs, only her next high. But to back it up, most addicts—and perhaps worrying is an addiction too?—begin early on to figure out coping skills because of difficulties in their lives. So even as children, they might find ways to get through their days lived in unsafe places with unsafe people, ways that morph as they grow up. One of the means of self-preservation and protection is to shut down the heart, to close off the valves of emotion because it hurts too much to feel.

For a child, the lack of empathy from others, compounded by one's own inability to care too much because of the sheer overwhelmingness of getting through each day whole, or at least alive, is the ideal setup for addiction. Children are too young and vulnerable to know any other way through, or out.

So addicts, and perhaps excessive worriers, have difficulty feeling empathy for others. And, it's critical to note, empathy for themselves.

Could worry be a substitute for action and for prayer? Once, on a radio program, my host said, "I've been praying a lot about that [issue]." Then she paused, looked me in the eye, hers deep and challenged. "No, that's not true," she said, "I haven't been praying. I have been dwelling on that problem, not praying about it."

I find it easier to worry than to pray, and even in the middle of praying, I start worrying. Worry becomes a substitute for living deeply and living by faith in an uncertain world. The passivity of worry takes over any effort to pray, to love, to act. In this way, perhaps, worry becomes an addiction, because it impedes our participation in life itself and genuinely loving others.

Psychologists might assert that when you act correctly, the associated emotions follow. A gifted couple we knew in our young married years, Art and Kathy, oversaw an enormous ministry to youth and hired a battalion of leaders to work in their summer program in an inner-city area. These mentors said, repeatedly, if you want to be enthusiastic, you have to act enthusiastic. Walk forward, act, and the reality and feelings will follow.

If worrying hinders or even obliterates empathy, then to feel empathic again, we need to act empathic. And the cycle continues, because as we act and then feel empathic, our worries decrease because we are not self-obsessing. We are blessing others through loving and serving them. Worry energy becomes serving energy, which begets more energy, and disrupts the worry cycle yet again.

This sounds good to me. Jesus' words have been bothering me immensely: when he talked about the sheep and the goats, and how when we serve "the least of these," we are serving him. When we feed the hungry, visit those in prison or in the hospital, house the homeless, clothe the naked, it is as though we are doing this for Christ (Matthew 25:31–46).

Mother Teresa of Calcutta understood this, and saw everyone she ministered to as Christ. She said, "There is always the danger that we may just do the work for the sake of the work. This is where the respect and the love and the devotion come in—that we do it to God, to Christ, and that's why we try to do it as beautifully as possible."

This challenges me. We don't want to make eye contact because someone might need more of us than we have to offer. And then others become an inconvenience when our worries occupy the whole viewfinder that is our life. Talk about myopic. Talk about sheep and goats. It's frightfully simple to just keep doing the next thing to get to the next place, and to never lift our eyes to realize that this is Jesus we are talking about; it is Jesus we are ignoring while ostensibly serving, doing the work for the sake of the work, as Mother Teresa said.

With ever-increasing burnout, our empathy steadily diminishes even while our worries skyrocket. Worry dehumanizes. But if we move toward empathy, toward loving others with Christ's love and seeing them *as* Christ, then we lose our self-focus, we begin to heal, but even more, the world around us begins to heal.

Inmates at Angola Penitentiary in Louisiana carry an average sentence of ninety-three years. Most will serve out their lives in the confines of those grounds, die there, and be buried in the cemetery with its white stones sticking out of the ground like a last, defiant uprising. Formerly known as the bloodiest prison in the U.S., Angola's atmosphere changed when Warden Burl Cain taught people to respect one another. One of the first rules put in place under his leadership was to forbid cursing from anyone—inmate, guard, and employee alike. This poured the groundwork for what would become the transformation of the ugliest, most fearsome prison in America.

The 2011 documentary *Serving Life*, narrated by Forest Whitaker, depicts the moving journey from death row to offering life to other inmates.[3]

The hospital has a hospice section staffed by paid professionals and served by volunteers. Volunteers, as in, inmates from the prison who have applied for the position and been screened extensively. They need a clean record in the prison, good behavior, cooperation, and no write-ups. But they also need something that they may not even know they have: heart.

The documentary follows the lives and work of several inmates who passed the screening and were accepted into the hospice program. The footage is gripping, as they serve others who are near death, as they learn to love again, as they give life to those who are dying, and in the process, find life for themselves. One hospice volunteer states that if they had been taught to care, they wouldn't have been in prison in the first place.

Assigned to patients bearing the sentence of death—patients who will die on the volunteers' watch, because no one is allowed to die alone—the volunteers learn to love in spite of fear, in spite of apathy, in spite of anger. In spite of difficult, unlovable patients. They learn to love.

They find a life they'd never known, a life they'd never learned about, a life they'd never believed possible. As they embrace that life, they reach out to estranged family members. One man hadn't spoken with his folks in years, even though his father had asked him to call every month. My husband and I wept as we watched his first phone call home, heard the joy in his parents' voices.

Learning to love. Empathy restored them to life, gave dignity and value to their patients, and rippled out beyond the walls to the outside.

A study by Helen Riess, MD, reports, "Evidence supports the physiological benefits of empathic relationships, including better immune function, shorter post-surgery hospital stays, fewer asthma attacks, stronger placebo response, and shorter duration of colds."[4]

Might there be a further psychology and a physiology to empathy, sort of like mothers who breastfeed their babies and get a dose of the feel-good oxytocin flooding their systems? Maybe empathy generates a feel-good hormone that comes from getting outside our own psychological entrapment, away from the prison bars of worry that constantly grid our view, and participating in another's life and circumstances. Perhaps that feel-good hormone is simply what many would call being alive.

Rather than the self-obsession that I find with worry, empathy invites me to look into another's eyes, and maybe even through their eyes.

I'm sick of my ultra-concern over my own well-being and that of people I love, sick of it dominating all that I think and do. And I wonder if worry is one of the most selfish occupations of my life.

This cannot be.

My red shoes need to trod some new ground. I need to walk into some other people's lives. I need to shod my feet with the gospel of peace.

Peace. Isn't that the opposite of worry?

My sticky-note friend listened as I poured another pitcherful of worry into the vat of airspace between us. Then, gentle as a feather, she inserted such kindness and direction: "I find that as I pray for someone I love, I begin to expand that prayer to others with the same problems. So when I pray for a loved one's difficult marriage, I then pray for others in painful relationship places, and then the circle widens to include their family and friends." In this way, her worry becomes prayer and then a telescope out of the tunnel of self-focus, out into the larger world. Worry leading to prayer leading to empathy.

Sometime later, on a brisk fall day with leaves rattling against windows and carpeting the pavement outside, I braked at the very edge of the stage, as close as I could get to the women without tumbling into their laps. Our day centered on their journeys: difficult, heartbreaking, disappointing, different than they imagined. There had been tears. Lots of laughter. Embracing. Praying around tables, in line, in the lobby. There had been acceptance. And yes, empathy. We had managed to see not just one another, but within one another, to see through another's eyes and to love well.

I recounted, there at the tip-end of the stage, the story of God calling Moses. Fearful, fleeing Moses, who for forty years had tried to forget or to distance himself or maybe to heal from his past. Moses, the octogenarian with the murder rap on his head. Moses, mountain man hidden away with his sheep, and then that bush that burned but wasn't consumed. Curious, this man crept forward toward the fire, and then the words: "Take off your sandals, for the place where you are standing is holy ground" (Exodus 3:5).

This place, right now, this moment, is holy. This place, with all its future worries and past pains and all the wounds embedded in our hearts, is holy.

Holding baskets, I invited the women to write on a piece of paper their commitment to this God who hallows even the hardest of places.

To declare this a holy spot to stand. And to take off their shoes, come forward, and place their commitments in the baskets as a love offering.

The first set of feet padded up to the stage, and this dear woman placed her offering of pain and hope, of worries relinquished, into the basket.

More, then more, feet. Bare feet. Funny-socked feet. Bad-toenail feet. Pedicured feet. Feet with polish on only their big toes because it's winter and who cares? Half socks, holey socks, no socks.

And the humbling act of removing our shoes, because we're so vulnerable, so naked. Our corns and thick nails and scaly skin and hammertoes exposed to the world. Dry skin and bunions visible, such defect, or neglect, or hardworking feet exposed.

But that very nakedness, that exposure, is the only gift we can bring to the table of relationships, to the table of God. That honesty that forms the bedrock for empathy, the common ground on which we all walk.

We walk across the room and find that we are not alone. And in the miracle of that embrace, we find our worries vanish. Vanish, vanquished, by the gift of empathy.

Consider the Wildflowers

To touch the soul of another human being
Is to walk on holy ground.

—Stephen Covey

By compassion we make others' misery our own, and so, by relieving them we relieve ourselves also.

—Sir Thomas Browne

Then Jesus made a circuit of all the towns and villages.
He taught in their meeting places, reported kingdom news,

and healed their diseased bodies, healed their bruised and
hurt lives.
When he looked out over the crowds, his heart broke.
So confused and aimless they were, like sheep with no
shepherd.
"What a huge harvest!" he said to his disciples.
"How few workers! On your knees and pray for harvest
hands!"

Matthew 9:35–38 THE MESSAGE

1. How have your worries isolated you from other people's pain?
   When have you experienced the commonalities of pain and
   bonded in a version of the Silent Walk?

2. If closing our emotional valves is a way to survive, then that
   gives worry all the more space to dominate. In what ways might
   worry be a coping skill that originated early in your life?

3. The Silent Walk isn't meant to induce guilt. Our cups run
   over with guilt. Rather, it's to invite us to expand our vision
   to include others, to recognize that pain is our great common
   denominator in this life on earth. How could you embrace
   others' pain in non-threatening, underwhelming ways?

4. It's not healthy to walk alone on this long, winding journey.
   Who walks beside you? What people have embraced you in
   your worry and pain? How often do you see them, and how
   might you make a regular discipline of companionship?

Votum

Jesus,
Your compassion
Moves me
Move into my soul
With that compassion
Open my eyes
To others' needs

And lift my eyes
From my own worries
To meet your eyes
And to see others
As you see them.
I want to weep
With those who weep
To help and hold those in pain
And to be held, as well.
Your grace is sufficient
And your arms are strong.
Enfold me now
Enable me to love
Now
And later.

Benedictus

Dear Child,
You have my heart
You always will
And I will pour myself into you
And then through you
Into this world
Yes weep with those who weep
And you will find that your heart
Fills over and over
With my love in you
Through you
And I will be enough for you.
Bruised and hurt lives
Need me.
Need you.
There is enough empathy
To go around.

9

Dance of the Fireflies

The Tool of Spontaneity

In the middle of a deep, dark night, a million fireflies weave and wink to silent music. The gift of freedom from worry and of spontaneous delight, as taught by my son.

The narrow back road bordered a preserve of walking paths and prairie grasses. As our son drove past in our ancient Suburban, the field glowed and winked. He pulled into the gravel parking lot, breathless at the sight.

The entire area pulsed with specks of light, millions of fireflies dancing in the dark midnight. Wonder so welled up in this son of ours, this spontaneous-burst-of-movement-and-joy son of ours, wonder so great that his breath caught up with his long limbs. In the purest form of awe, he began to turn and leap and whirl amongst the fireflies.

Joy. In a field. At midnight.

For those minutes, wonder swallowed worry. He entered into a bit of eternity. I've never forgotten that image, as he told it to me later. My heart catches a little in my throat, a stutter of longing, a tightening of my child-heart that says, "Me, too! I want to see fireflies. I want to spin amongst them. I want to be so moved by beauty that I participate—play!—in the midst of the miracle."

Life is serious, and then we die. But meanwhile, maybe we could learn how to relieve the pressure of a worry-filled life, to push back at the walls of expectation that close in upon us. Maybe we, too, could spot a firelit night and learn to be present.

Not just present, though.

To participate in that glory.

Growing up, of course, is a pretty serious responsibility, and once those bills start coming in our name, life changes. The entire game changes. No more play dates arranged by kind and helpful parents. No more lazy summer days of staring at the sky and dreaming, although perhaps that was several generations ago and something extinct, forced out of existence by the pollution of pressure to get kids into the best colleges and off on their best footing and launched into the world with solid and strategic planning.

But didn't Jesus say, "Become like little children" (Matthew 18:3)? This week, as I read the Gospels (for instance, see Mark 12:37), I was struck by the response of the listeners as Jesus preached. They were delighted. Delighted? Isn't that a little over the top? Isn't this world too serious for that? If we're all headed down the wide and paved highway to hell, then delighting people with our exposition of life and Scripture seems to be a lavishness of the worst kind. Like feeding a child soda pop in a bottle for his entire infancy— how fun, the child thinks, this is sweet and wonderful—and then inducing brain damage.

Wait, though. This is Jesus we're talking about. Jesus, who delighted his audience by the intersection of life and God, and God's Word. Jesus, who mesmerized people with truth and grace, with joy and kindness, with a love bigger than anyone had ever known before, a love wider than blue sky and blue sea combined. This Jesus freed a woman long bound by both religiosity and infirmity, and the reaction? The religious leaders were humiliated and bitter and outraged at the sheer profligacy of healing (as though healing were an extravagance, as though it could be regulated to a certain day of the week!), but the people, the common everyday you-and-me kind of folks? They "were delighted with all the wonderful things he was doing" (Luke 13:10–17).

Jesus had seen it all. Seen the thick darkness, before speaking the world into existence. Seen a beauty beyond anything our feeble minds can imagine, beauty without the veil that's now pulled between us and creation. Jesus stood at the top of mountains, hung the stars in space, created the vast panorama of color and depth, the brilliance of the life in the rich oceans, the vibrant color of the corals and the great blue whale, the flashlight fish and the electric eel. Jesus knew the essence—and the essential-ness—of life itself.

Yes, yes, a thousand nods of amen. But Jesus also saw the depth of depravity, far too soon after the beginning of night and day, the first day, the second day, the third day. He saw the very life strangled out of the people created in that first week, the people designed to be the pinnacle of God's creativity. Jesus saw the seriousness from the very beginning, the snuffing out of the flame that is life, delight. He witnessed it all, and it was like killing off the coral. It must have hurt him in every cell of his heart. Grief must have blanketed his joy, suffocating it like rain on a campfire.

And when he came to earth, he didn't pound the pulpit and preach hellfire all the time. Some of the time, maybe. But all the time? Nope. Some of the time, he delighted people with his words. Delighted them. Look at the lilies of the field! A camel going through the eye of a needle. People probably held their sides in laughter at some of his word pictures. And the works he did: Water into wine! Strolling across the water. Imagine! That's some crazy stuff.

Thinking about that firefly night, no doubt God enjoys watching all his handiwork, just the holy trio of Father, Son, Holy Spirit, like some heavenly audience clapping from the nosebleed section. But they didn't produce such a masterpiece for their own sake. Surely they created all that glory so that we could participate in it, so that we could be eyewitnesses of such masterworks and be literally swept off our feet.

Surely that night in the field alight with fireflies, God noticed our son noticing, stopping, and then playing in the glory, and God rejoiced. God whirled with him in that field.

That's what I want. I want the sense of God whirling with me in the fields, spinning with me in the firefly nights. I want to live without the manacles of worry chaining me to my tasks and my fear. I want to live, really live.

Otherwise, worry wins.

This cannot be, friends. We cannot allow worry to win. Because if worry wins, it's all for naught. The world around us. The intensity of color, of creation. The beauty. Life itself.

If worry wins, it's all for naught.

So bring on the fireflies.

Lovely, you say, arms folded across your chest, nodding in a serious and godly fashion. But life is too important to waste time. We have work to do. Yes, life *is* serious. Responsibilities *are* real. And if life is to go on, then we have to get on with it all. The lists. The pushing. The work of making life happen.

Except . . . since when do we have so much power that we actually make life happen? It seems to me that either we enter into the life happening all around us, a little like launching a canoe in a sweetly running stream and putting our paddles in and cooperating with the current—or we can throw ourselves like a giant rock into the middle. Either way, we don't make the current happen. The current of life flows, and we can join in, using good paddling techniques and canoeing wisdom, and hope for some nice splashing along the way, or we can be a great big bully rock refusing to be moved.

I don't want to be a rock in the middle of the river, life splashing past me and around me for the rest of my days or the bulk of my minutes. Worry turns me into a stodgy rock. It's like planting my giant desk in the middle of a playground and getting on with my serious business.

I'm not advocating life as a perpetual visit to the circus, the amusement park, and the corner bar. But if worry turns me into a stone, I will never really live.

There is a work-around to this dilemma. God turns hearts of stone to flesh again. God makes dry bones dance.

Play is becoming extinct even for children, I'm afraid, taken over by organized sports and structured activities. Tell me this: When did you stop playing? Or did you ever play? What was your favorite form of play as a five-year-old? Do you even remember, or is there someone you could ask? What about when you were eight? Do you still know the rules for Kick the Can? When did you last toss a Frisbee or play Ghost in the Graveyard? How long has it been since you pushed the pedals on a real bike and felt the wind in your hair and the elation of almost flying? The last time you toasted a marshmallow over the flame of your gas burner and burned your tongue on the tines of the fork but licked the sweet stuff off your lips with joy?

When is the last time you took off your shoes and ran or walked about barefoot in the dew-damp grass? Or blew dandelion fluff (in someone else's yard, preferably), or set off a few bottle rockets? Or sat under the night sky, quiet, watching the moon and stars gather on stage for their nightly one-of-a-kind performance?

Why are these only acceptable for people of a certain age? My fear is that if we wait until we retire to swirl among the fireflies, we might not live long enough to retire.

Maybe I'm getting ahead of myself.

Fireflies diminish in number every year, confused by the artificial light of our technological advances. In natural darkness, lightning bugs begin to pulse in rhythm, a syncopated flash dance. With their twinkling light, they call to one another, answer one another. But a passing car's headlights throw off the fireflies, in both their rhythm and mating. Scientists suspect this may be part of the lower lightning bug population.

I suspect that the intrusion of technology means worry is always at our fingertips, confusing us and confusing our bodies' natural healing mechanisms. Year after year, we diminish in soul and spirit, in vibrancy and vitality. We no longer realize that the longing in our soul, the deep ache in our heart, is related to the loss of joy, of spontaneity. Worries extinguish the pulse of our faith. There are so few places where we can twirl.

Just as with salsa dancing, though, we run smack into the shield of armor that says Good Christian Women spend their lives doing good works, with God's help and to God's glory. Amen to that. But in the days before man discovered electricity, no one stayed up all night long working and doing good things. They slept; they put their feet up on a log around the campfire and strummed guitars; they sang impromptu songs from their sleeping bags. They went for walks at dusk, held hands under the stars, sat on the beach at dawn and watched the sun rise and the manta rays joy-jump and slap the surface in crazy belly flops. There was room for relaxation, room for rest, room for quietude and gentle kindness. Room for healing.

Another shield we hoist in front of our chests, or our culture throws subtly in front of us, is that Good Christian Women are busy women. If we aren't busy we aren't valuable. If we aren't busy, we aren't doing good works and we aren't building up the kingdom.

We aren't caring about the world, aren't caring for hearth and home and those inhabiting it.

Then again, I wonder if we give God glory when we collapse from heart palpitations or develop some worry-related condition—or ruin our relationships because we are preoccupied with our niggling enemy, worry.

Sometimes it isn't anyone else's expectations that drive us. It isn't about the standards we inherited by the way we were raised, or those passed on by our boss or spouse or friend. (Although I do have friends who cannot abide the thought of a jigsaw puzzle, a game of Scrabble, or even a good novel, because their mothers refused to play games or read for pleasure. So role modeling is relevant.)

We can't blame anyone else for our life as it is, not any longer. That's one of the facts we need to make clear to ourselves, right now. We are adults, and our past no longer needs to control us. We drive ourselves about, demanding a higher standard for ourselves than God does. Remember, God stopped to sit back and clap after each day of creation, to leap up and down and say, "Whoa, this is good! Good! Good! Very good!"

What if you didn't finish the to-do list you had composed for today? What if you don't finish it tomorrow, either? Will the world stop, the earth fall off its axis, the moon fling itself out of orbit and out into space?

Who, after all, established the rule that said playtime ends after you start kindergarten? Who decided that we no longer have the right to appreciate the world around us, that it is an extravagance?

Maybe we don't even believe that ourselves. What could possibly be wrong with a walk in the park? Well, we might say it'd be better if it were the Museum of Science and Industry, because then we would be learning, feeding our brains. See what happens? If we don't get double return on our investments, then we think we need to rethink them.

We can't afford this belief system. It crushes us with its over-wrought expectations, with its circuit-breaking worry.

Scientists also speculate that the loss of natural habitat inhibits the fireflies' reproduction. Lightning bugs love long, wavy grasses and spend their days hanging out, bobbing about in the breeze or sheltering in the blades. But neighbors don't like our long, wavy grasses, so we get out high-powered lawn mowers every week and hack off the tops. This probably doesn't help the lightning bugs much.

Controlling impressions is behind some of our worry, I think. If we are honest, we often push ourselves because we seek success, there is fierce competition, and we want people to like us. (I have met very few exceptions to this rule. If you are one, please get in touch with me. I want to interview you, or better yet, be your friend.) Worry is a useless attempt at control, but it's like manicuring the lawn. We maintain some form of control if we worry, otherwise we might look irresponsible. Non-worriers are suspicious to us worriers, who think, *What is wrong with you? You should be worried and because you aren't, you must be callused. You must not care. You are not taking life seriously, and life is serious. Buck up.* So we cut the grass, and the fireflies in our souls die off.

Control and worry seem like BFFs.

Worry eats into our souls' bone marrow, weakening us from the inside out like osteoporosis. We end up with an extensive interior latticework, holes and more holes leaving us vulnerable to a break, or a breakdown. What if bone-building, soul-building recovery looked like discovery? Discovery of delight, of play.

Fireflies know the art of hanging out, of living in life-giving spots. They love puddles and rotting logs, humidity and warmth.

When the sun drops below the horizon and the stars begin to blink in the sky, at just the right time, they light up the night.

If they do not, they will die off.

So, I'm afraid, will we.

She was an impish brunette and six years old.[1] We met at church. There, after the service, several of us clustered in a group, I the only mother with grown children. The other moms still had birds in the nest, some of them scarcely with feathers, let alone flying and sometimes free falling.

This little elf planted herself in the center of us women, smiling. Then she started twirling in a circle between us, just circling like a ballerina, practicing her turns. Her mother tried to still her, and the child covered her face by putting her hood on backwards, then spinning some more.

"Stop twirling," her mother said. "You'll fall down."

I wondered about that, whether the mother was really worried about her child falling, or about her becoming the center of attention, or disturbing the peace. And I wondered whether the child would really fall down, this little girl so much closer to the ground, so much more centered, than we were. We wise adults who want so much to control our worlds and not have children make us—*ahem*—look bad in the process.

One of my many mistakes as a mother has been attempting to control my children lest they disturb others, when they were only being children, doing childlike stuff. Like spinning into adult conversations that are stiflingly boring to a kid needing to know she, too, exists in a circle of women.

Belatedly, I'm recognizing the wisdom of allowing kids to find their limits in safety, with small decisions and small consequences, rather than waiting until they fly the coop and crash in a big way. Twirling in church in a circle of women seemed a safe way to experience risk and safety. I, the new adult to the church and to this group, suggested to this slight child, "Why don't you see what happens if you keep spinning?"

"No, don't listen to Mrs. Rubietta," her mother said. "I want you to stop spinning."

Appalled, I realized I'd trespassed her authority. A new acquaintance, I wasn't the child's mother or even her mother's friend, and had no business (or intention of) inviting defiance.

"Please listen to your mother, honey," I said, a tad late noticing the context. And to the mother, "Please forgive me. I didn't mean to suggest disobedience or usurp your authority."

And I didn't know the full story. Though she behaved like an angel throughout the church service, maybe the child spun out of control daily and her mother constantly had to reel her in, wind her back up into the nest. Maybe at six the child had such a twirling streak that she could never sit still, couldn't stop long enough to listen or learn, to help, to be part of the life around her.

But later, I felt sad, sad for the little girl who couldn't twirl in church. One of the gifts we can give, as adults in the body of Christ, is acceptance and the ability to be childlike. I can't imagine a safer place to twirl, in a sanctuary and right inside a circle of women who love you and think you're adorable. I hope she can find other spinning places to experience the dizzying delight of childlikeness, the joy of a world that circles you, if only for a moment. And arms to catch you when—not if, but when—you fall.

Somehow, I think Jesus would smile if he caught us twirling in church, twirling for the sake of sheer joy, because we're alive and so is he. And he'd catch us if we fell, stand us back up on our feet.

Maybe it's time to add some torque into our lives. To find the rules for Kick the Can, or kick off our shoes and make footprints in the sand, or the dewy grass. To dance among the fireflies. People might disapprove, but if that kills us, at least we will die happy, filled with delight, remembering what cool green feels like on our hot souls.

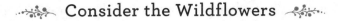

Consider the Wildflowers

Saw butterflies dancing
yesterday
over and over they twirled
and spun
air ballerinas in the morning
sun
It is spring
They are free
The old is gone
The new is come

Blessed are the people who know the passwords of praise,
who shout on parade in the bright presence of God.
Delighted, they dance all day long;
they know who you are, what you do—they can't keep it
quiet!
Your vibrant beauty has gotten inside us—you've been so
good to us!
We're walking on air!
All we are and have we owe to God, Holy God of Israel,
our King!

Psalm 89:15–18 THE MESSAGE

1. Recall some firefly moments, in your journal or in conversation with God—moments of sheer spontaneity in your life. What was happening, and how did you abandon worry and protocol? What did you do with the worry?

2. What do you think about Jesus delighting his listeners? How does this fit with your image of the Savior of all? When have you experienced the delight of Jesus, and where?

3. When do you worry that worry will win? What threatens to push you over the edge into that abyss? How does technology

138

make you more susceptible to worry? In what ways are you seeing it diminish your vitality, or others'? In what ways are the need to control and worry BFFs in your life?

4. Make a list of the places you can twirl. Who or what would stop you from slipping them into slots on your calendar? Who are some twirling friends?

Votum

Jesus,
I'd love to be delighted
In your love
But it's still hard
To believe
You delight in me
And that you delighted
Your listeners
And that you delighted
To create the world
And you delighted
To create me.
Honestly.
If that were true
I could twirl
Straight to heaven
And we could spin
Forever.

Benedictus

Child,
Hear me on this
You are my delight
It is my great joy
To create fireflies
And flowers

And hang the stars
In the sky
For you
For me
For us.
And to see you
Delighting in all
I have made
Delights me.
I'd love to see you twirl
To see that little girl
in you
Spin to the surface
And worship me
In a burst of joy.
Let the children
Come
To me.

10

School Pictures
The Tool of Identity

The worst and the funniest and what we see in the
mirror. And the wonder of wonders, the great eradicator
of worry: Someone delights in us.

One by one, they climbed the stairs to the overly bright stage. Camera crews rolled closer, pulled back, panned the wildly cheering crowd (even though we, the crowd, which included my daughter and me, did not know why we cheered).

The audience obeyed the applause signs with gusto as the talk show host introduced the three guests. Behind them, three enormous easels stood with giant canvases hiding the displays beneath.

Turns out, these were the winners (or losers, depending on your view) of a photo contest: Send in your worst school picture and we will pick the three worst of the worst and give you a free trip to our show so that you can feel mortified remembering how hideous you looked as a child on picture day.

Not only that, but we will laugh at you, laugh until tears run down our faces, laugh at the jokes the show host cracks, laugh at your expense. It's all in good fun—well, for us, if not for you—and it's good for ratings and ratings are good for us.

So send in your pictures.

People did. At least, three people did, and these adults now stood before us all on the hard and polished stage in the harsh light of a Hollywood ratings game.

These astounding photos framed some of the worst days of those kids' lives. Two of the pictures were from high school, the young man looking like a lawn mower had taken out the top of his hair and left the sides to ready themselves for takeoff. The third-grader won the trauma test, though: home perm gone bad (Brillo-pad bad), smashed down with a comb to a fine frizz that brushed the top rim of oversized bottle-bottom glasses.

The contest left me feeling gloomy. Sure, it was a relief to know that the children had outgrown their photos and matured into responsible, nice-looking people. At any rate, they'd outgrown their looks in the photos. But do we ever outgrow the cost of being a child?

We were children, and picture day was the worst day of the year, unless you counted Valentine's Day, or the day when everyone but you got invited to the popular kid's birthday party.

Remember? Was there ever a good day to be a child on picture day? Your hair never worked right; the pixie haircut was lopsided yet again, because moms didn't know how to work with those goofy cowlicks. Arrgh! And the clothes: that hideous blouse, or your clothes weren't new, or even worse, were hand-me-downs. No matter what, your best friend looked like someone from a magazine, and you looked only slightly better than your worst nightmare.

Sometimes it isn't the image we see in the yearbook that we best remember. It's the child we imagine, with the wistful combination of hope and laughter and perhaps a smidgen of sadness. It's hard to see around the photographer's lighting, but behind the gleam in our eyes is a reality check: Childhood is a bitter-sweet mixture of fireflies and mosquitoes, and sometimes the mosquitoes win.

Though the people on the TV show appeared stable, it's hard to know the cost of leaving that child behind. To simply move forward, relieved that our hair works better now or that we wear contacts or that we no longer look as though our parents beamed us in from outer space.

Remember holding it together all the way through the school day, and then dragging into the house in relief, like you'd evaded the taunting voices one more time? And then, inside the relative safety (or perhaps non-safety; not everyone comes home to a haven) of your house, you shattered into a bunch of broken pieces? So much pressure, being a child in a world of extremely high expectations.

Sometimes, just getting into the doorway of our home isn't enough. Sometimes, there's no safe place to dissolve into childlike worry, no place to cleanse and nurse the wounds. It's possible we could blame someone for that, possible but not helpful. However, those wounds internalize, little thorns buried into the palms of our souls.

Before long, we figure out how to appear acceptable, how to look like we have it all together, whatever *that* is. We figure out what our teachers, our parents expect of us (whether we decide to comply or not). We begin to build an image of ourselves that leaves the honest little girl behind, the one with the giant eyes, taking in the whole world and not knowing how to digest it.

We no longer honestly know who we are. That giant-eyed child still lives within us, and when the world feels bigger than we are, we worry. When the problems in life seem larger than our family safety or coping skills, we worry. When our resources show up as debits rather than credits, we worry. And when the chasm of what we show to the world and what we know about ourselves on the inside broadens, we worry. Because one day we will be found out.

And then, the sheer pace of our life eclipses the hope of healing. Healing becomes a luxury—inviting that little girl into healing, an impossibility, compounding the grieving worry-weight we carry.

A television show might not be the best place to re-encounter yourself at a young age. It's one thing to make fun of ourselves. It's another to let someone else do that for us on national television.

Say you find a picture of yourself as a child at six or eight years old. Or maybe several pictures from your youth. Cozy up in a quiet place, with a journal or some other means of tracking your thoughts, memories, and feelings.

What do you remember most? Your clothes, the friends, what it felt like to go to school? Recess, gym class? Teachers? Sunday school? Did you ride the bus, walk, carpool? Were you home-schooled? What do you remember—good or bad?

Were you happy? Sad? Did you laugh a lot, feel worried or stressed? What dreams did you have for the future? What did you love to do? Where did you feel safe, comfortable, or both? What are some of the messages you told yourself, or others told you *about* you?

Maybe part of our worry problem today is that we have lost the pictures of ourselves at a young age: impressionable, hopeful, dreaming (even if adults discouraged it). Have we lost the little girl who laughed and cried and forgave easily, who healed quickly? What good parts rise to your memory? Can you list them?

Is there a list of your shortcomings too? All those times when you knew your inadequacies like you knew your own name? What about responsibilities, rules? Were you the good girl, the straight-A girl, the don't-let-anyone-get-upset girl, the funny girl whose job was to make everyone else laugh? The peacekeeper, the problem-solver, the family baggage carrier, the scapegoat, the black sheep?

We've had a lifetime to learn to worry. Maybe we can take time to notice, to re-engage that little girl we once were, and to recover.

"Let us hope that we are all preceded in this world by a love story."[1]

This quote appears at the beginning of the award-winning movie *Sweet Land*, a haunting, beautiful story of love, acceptance, community, and identity in post-World War II America.

Let us hope, indeed, that we are all preceded by a love story. But our experience so often bears witness to a different reality. Yes, many of us were born of loving parents and raised in nurturing homes. But many were not. Some of us were deeply loved, some were not. Some of us felt that deep love, some of us did not.

Regardless of the circumstances of our birth, we understand at an early age that love has very little to do with acceptance, that someone else defines the rules for that exclusive club, and most of us were not issued an invitation.

Since playground days, we've learned that we don't always have what it takes. Our insufficiencies, like a minor chord in the background of our lives, play nonetheless, crescendoing at awkward moments and overpowering the melody line we're trying to sing, or pretending to sing, or perhaps humming in a tuneless breath.

This certainty of our inadequacy adds to the undertone of worry constantly plucking the strings of our soul.

Some of us still feel like the kid in the worst-picture contest in terms of our appearance. Particularly women carry that message of not measuring up, and it shows in our faces. We are our own glass ceiling. We don't need anyone else to cap our potential. We can manage that by ourselves.

But we also worry about our measurements, and how those don't measure up, either. Very few women I know are delighted with their weight, shape, or face, or much else about their physical appearance. Some don't even look in the mirror. Some do, and seriously dislike what they see. We enforce a gag order on this, though, knowing it is "unspiritual" to worry about how we look, and it is also "unspiritual" to be pleased with how we look! Not a win-win.

A tape measure is not our bottom line. Our lives are measured more like liquid, which expands to fill its container. Every single day, our job is simply to live well in the space we occupy in this world. To live well in our body, however ample the hips or small the bustline. To fill the space that is us, to fill it to the brim.

Though our worries weigh us down, Scripture compares these to mere feathers or flakes of snow. They blow away in the wind and melt in the sun when compared to the celebration that is coming:

> We do not lose heart. Though outwardly we are wasting away, yet inwardly we are being renewed day by day. For our light and momentary troubles are achieving for us an eternal glory that far outweighs them all.
>
> 2 Corinthians 4:16–17

This perspective lifts us beyond our worries and into wonder that God can convert our troubles into glory.

And while we wait this side of glory, consider this: The Scriptures tell us that Christ in us is our hope of glory (Colossians 1:27). That's how we fill this space well: We fill ourselves up, to the brim, with Christ. Day after day, when the worries threaten to strangle the tiny seeds of faith in our heart, we turn back to Jesus and open our hearts like a cup and invite him to pour himself into us. All those promises of filling: filled with fruit, with laughter, with awe, with knowledge, with joy, with love, with hope.[2] *Filled.*

How do we do that? We pore over the Scriptures, hold on to a verse a day or even a phrase. We find our favorite hymns or praise songs and sing those words, that truth, so that the worried little girl inside us hears and receives comfort. We repeat aloud the truth, smack in the face of our worries: We are found by Christ, we are claimed by Christ, we are loved by Christ, we are filled by Christ. He is our hope; he is our standard of measure.

The picture haunts me. The men could be from the local church softball team, the back row standing, the front row kneeling or squatting. Every single person in the photo looks like a neighbor, someone I've met on an airplane, a pastor of a church. Nothing about them would stop my husband or me from inviting one of them home for dinner. Nothing distinguishes these gentlemen from anyone else on the street or in the grocery store.

Except their numbers.

Each of these men is a convict, and they play softball on a prison team. Their sentences have dwindled to a work camp, and the next stop is a halfway house, or for most of them, an ankle monitor. And every day for the rest of their lives, their unspoken or spoken dossier will come with a number. Their prisoner identification number.

For two days, I've looked at this picture, stared at the men, prayed for them. They are dear to my heart, though I know only one of them by name. They are dear to my heart, and they break my heart, and they give certainty to my heart.

They are dear to me because they are dear to Jesus. That may sound pious, but Jesus said if we love the prisoner, we love him. I love these men because one of them is all of them. I pray for them, for their families, for their futures and hopes and wounds and all that life has cost them. I pray for their cell mates, for the prison guards, wardens, and other employees.

I pray for them because these convicts—if we must label them—remind me of me. Of you. Of every person sitting with us in church or at the truck stop. For aren't we all convicts, born broken into a broken world, fugitives from the law? Are they not a picture of us all?

God has our number, knows it by heart. And here is where certainty comes to my heart, to my worry-flattened heart and haunted eyes. Certainty for all of us.

God knows our number, and it's not a prison number. This is the conviction for me. God knows us as we are, as we have been. Knows the deep worry of our lives, knows that worry deforms us spiritually and emotionally, wreaks havoc on our relationships.

He knows all this, but still numbers us—counts us—among the loved. We are part of the beloved, and that is what I desperately want to live into. That is what I want those men in that picture to know. That absolutely nothing separates us from them. We are broken and we are loved. Not because we've lived exemplary lives. Not one of us has, save one: Jesus.

The men in the picture give me certainty, a positive ID. Because they are more than a number. They are more than their prison record. They are more than the deeds of their past.

If they aren't, then we are all sunk. They have served their time. But we have not.[3]

They were charged; we were not. They haven't done a thing that we might not have done in the same circumstances, all things being equal. But they were caught. Some of us were and some of us were not. Maybe we didn't externalize the crime like they did. Maybe no one got hurt except us, because we only thought rather than acted on the thought. But there is no reason we are not there, serving time, having our picture taken under a gigantic shade tree with two rows of comrades, holding a winners' plaque.

In this sideways world, where wounds bring out the worst in us and—if we wait long enough and work hard enough—can bring out the best in us, we all come out broken. We all come out of the womb fearfully and wonderfully made, and then something goes wrong.

Though it might not be an external abnormality, we are all born with a birth defect: We are broken in soul, and all our lives, all our worrying lives, that brokenness will be our biggest bane and perhaps our biggest blessing. The worries that trail after us like the long shadows of evening (never leaving us until we lie down in a pine box or the sun falls from the sky) are the shards that draw blood and remind us that we need healing.

Our worries convict us. The tracks between our brows convict us. We are convicts, and one conviction is this: that we are not enough, that the sum of our parts is inadequate, and even worse, that God is not enough for us. God might not take care of us. God might not love us enough to rescue us.

There. I have tapped it out in black on white.

Now that we know that much of the truth, we can fill in the long black gaping blanks with the rest of the truth. Because that is not the end of the story; it isn't even the beginning of the story. The photo shoot began long ago, before third grade, before our birth, even before the birth of the world, when God "chose us in him before the creation of the world," as Paul writes in Ephesians 1:4. Before the creation of the world! Before we'd burst onto the scene in blood and brokenness, before we'd had a chance to display our wounds to the world at large. Before we had a chance to be further wounded by the world around us.

Long before that, before Christ spoke the world into existence, before God colored in the lines with sky blue and seafoam green. Before all that, God chose us.

In the great contest that would become our life, the haves and the have-nots, the dos and the do-nots, God chose us. God picked us for the team. The little girl inside me jumps up and down at this. God picked me! God picked you!

Our identity formed before the clock started ticking, before sperm and egg met, before passion flamed. Our identity, formed in the heart of God. "I choose you," God said.

But God didn't stop there. God shaped us, formed us in our mother's womb; we are fearfully and wonderfully made (see Psalm 139). Imagine that! In this world where our worries separate us from all the successful and faithful people around us, God says you are "wonderfully made." And about all those worry-words that clutter our brains and our prayer journals, all the worry beads that we grip with the gnarled hands of our hearts—God knows every word before it's even on our tongues (see Psalm 139).

Every word. Every worry.

And more than that. God says in Isaiah 49:16, "I have engraved you on the palms of my hands; your walls are ever before me." And "no one can snatch [you] out of my Father's hand" (John 10:29).

Nothing. Not our worries. Not our deformity of soul that says, *You aren't enough, I'm not enough, nothing is enough.* Not even the conviction that we are convicts.

Our prison picture? Disappearing ink.

Because God said, "There is now no condemnation for those who are in Christ Jesus" (Romans 8:1). Because God said, "You are precious and honored in my sight, and because I love you . . ." (Isaiah 43:4).

Our identity, born in the heart of God before the birth of the earth, becomes the key to our emancipation from the prison of worry.

"Let us hope that we are all preceded in this world by a love story."
Yes indeed.
But that is more than a hope.
That's a fact.
A love story from eternity past, all the way to eternity future.
And all the days in between.

And for today, for this precious moment of now, we relish the delight of God choosing us. Delighting in us. Us.

The worries will return, but we will melt them again, moment by moment, in the warmth of the Son.

Consider the Wildflowers

You must learn to understand that all your deficiencies,
even those that come from your past sins and vicious
habits,
are part of my loving providence for you,
and that it is just with those deficiencies, just the way you
are now, that I would love you.
Therefore you must overcome the habit of judging how you
would make yourself acceptable to me.
When you do this you are putting your providence, your
wisdom before mine.
It is my wisdom that tells you, "The way you are acceptable to me, the way I want to love you, is the way you
are now, with all your defects and deficiencies.
I could wipe them out in a moment if I wanted to,
but then I could not love you the way I want to love you,
the way you are—now."[4]

—Julian of Norwich, *Revelations of Divine Love*

Oh yes, you shaped me first inside, then out;
you formed me in my mother's womb.
I thank you, High God—you're breathtaking!
Body and soul, I am marvelously made!
I worship in adoration—what a creation!
You know me inside and out,
you know every bone in my body;
You know exactly how I was made, bit by bit,
how I was sculpted from nothing into something.

Psalm 139:13–15 THE MESSAGE

1. Find a picture of yourself as a child. What do you see? Memories of that time, messages you'd already begun to live into? How has that time shaped your identity? What has it cost you to abandon that child and turn into a grown-up?

2. What relationship do you see between the giant-eyed child you were and the things you worry about today? How is worry related to the powerlessness of that child? What about the chasm between the person you show to the world and the person you know to be yourself? How often do you feel like a fraud, and how do you cover that up?

3. What are you most afraid of? Who you really are? That you are a number only, not part of the beloved? How hard is it to believe that you are loved as is, that your past and present failures do not render you a convict, but rather a person defined by God's love and grace? When do you experience that?

4. If you fill yourself full of Jesus, where does your worry go? How can you fill the space that is you well? What ways might you practice filling yourself?

Votum

Dear Jesus,
Could you please
Change my ID
Make me
ID me
Find me.
Unfreeze the frame
Frozen at failure
And lead me to
The Name that is higher
Than mine.
Correct my vision

That I might see your love
For me
And believe your love
For me
And live in who you
Call me to be.
Convict me
And set me free.
I am more than a prison number.
I am numbered among
Your beloved.

Benedictus

Dear Daughter,
You are more than your picture
At any given time
And I see you
Not frozen in time
In the awkwardness
Of halfway there
Not a freeze frame
Of social gaffes
And all the failures
You seem to remember.
I see you as my child
I see you stamped with
"Made in My Image"
I see you
As my beloved
And in you
I am
Well pleased.
Because you are in Christ
And Christ is One
With Me
And you are looking

More and more
Like us.
May you find your freedom
In that conviction
In that judgment
That declaration
Child of God

11

Fly Crew

The Tool of Trust

Peter Pan's harness and [her] personal flyer. And . . . the God who commands his angels to guard you in all your ways. If you stumble they'll lift you up in their hands (see Psalm 91:11–12). A worry-free flight is possible . . . one second at a time.

Backstage, cast and crew buzzed in the semidarkness. The fly crew was here, ready for flight training. It was hot, stifling, humid, and frightening—to me at least. When the word spread—the school would hire a professional team to train *Peter Pan*'s cast members to fly—excitement stampeded through the auditions. Only a few lucky people would be harnessed and trained, but oh, the joy! The thrill! The great adventure.

A key rule for this kind of flying is that your personal flyer be 100 percent trustworthy; it helps if that person has a vested interest in the cast member who would take to the air. Peter Pan's personal flyer: her father.

I watched the two of them together, the father committed to keeping his daughter safe and alive and also helping her fly—perhaps the single greatest challenge of a parent. And the daughter, absolutely confident that her daddy could be entrusted with her life. He showed up, every single rehearsal and performance, faithful to keep her safe and keep her flying.

Though cables and pulleys would be very visible backstage, the audience would be swept up in the mystery, all the machinations out of sight. But never, not for one second, would Peter Pan or Tinker Bell or any of the other flying characters be without their personal flyer, never would they be left unattended. Never. Not ever.

Though I've worked at overcoming my very slight fear of heights (yes, we can add that to my neuroses), the idea of free floating in the sky unhinges me a bit. Hang gliding? Probably not. Those little wobbly planes called ultralights, popular in rural areas (and with a fairly high mortality rate)? No. Partly because I've lived with enough risk, I think; I don't need to seek it out.

In fact, because life in this season feels so wobbly, I seldom pursue risk at all. But there's a limit to how much safety I can legislate. I try: I've forged a rickety system of margin, a means of staying safe. With worry and work trampling my family like an army marching through the flower garden, crowding in extra commitments hit my don't-even-think-about-it list. I stopped volunteering, stopped reaching out, quit making "just checking in" calls to friends. No "Grab a coffee?" invitations. I stopped talking on the phone while preparing dinner because distraction plus the clock, plus kids and their activities, and oh, yes, needs, plus the seasoning of ADHD, plus the irritation and stress of being too distracted, plus a kink in my neck, plus distraction—wait, I said that already—well, I had to choose. A little bit of margin meant protection of my scarcest commodity, time, and became a means of both legislating safety and limiting risk.

This worked, somewhat, in terms of guarding my time and the relationships I treasured most in the world. At least I wasn't volunteering for extra duty on the insanity shift. That margin kept me safer but also left me without ballast, no one pulling the cable to lift me up. Not having those people in place meant a long, slow leak of the helium of comradeship and accountability and challenge—and before long, no flying, no friends.

One day, as I raced from a store and unlocked my car door, heaving groceries into the back seat, I distinctly heard that faint voice that I know doesn't come from my own brain because I wouldn't have thought of it: "You have made an idol of safety."

I climbed into the Suburban and leaned back, my heart *patumping* in my chest.

An idol of safety?

First I wanted to be angry and defensive. But it's hard to argue with that Voice. Well, it's easy to argue, but the only way to win in that little tussle is to listen deeply and, ultimately, to agree.

The opposite of safety is danger. Risk. I wait with that, now, because there is an untruth buried beneath the assumption, first of all, that we can keep ourselves safe. That is a lie.

Safety is like trying to live without stress; without stress, whether good or bad, we start to decay. Maybe there's no such thing as stasis. We either move forward or move backward. And if we really think we are maintaining some status quo by worrying, that we are somehow keeping ourselves safe, then we are delusional. Trying to stay safe is dangerous.

Dangerous for soul. For body. For mind. For life.

Peter Pan would never learn to fly if she decided to stay safe. And, in a lovely juxtaposition, by taking the risk and learning to fly with her personal flyer, she flew without injury or hazard. But more than that: The elation of flying, even on a limited stage set, of soaring from above and swooping across the stage—well, nothing compares. For those brief seconds in the air, those un-fettered, boundless moments, she was more alive than ever in her life.

A recent headline boasted, "Personal jetpacks near approval for use." I'm sure loads of people who have loads of money will invest in their very own jetpack ASAP. There's probably a waiting list. But without a jetpack, our bodies aren't designed for flying. If we were supposed to fly, we would look like birds, with broad strong wings, feathers, aerodynamic bodies, legs growing out of our tummies and easily tucked against us in flight. Either we were a mistake in design or we were designed for the ground, for earth. Victims of both gravity and ergonomics.

Our bodies aren't created for flying, but our souls are. The Scriptures tell us, "Those who hope in the Lord will renew their strength. They will soar on wings like eagles; they will run and not grow weary, they will walk and not be faint" (Isaiah 40:31). How do we do this?

It's Peter Pan and her personal flyer.

It's us—and the entire battalion of helps God gives us for our journey toward heaven.

It's the opposite of worry.

In one word: trust.

Tears needled my eyes when I learned that Peter Pan's personal flyer was her father. Her daddy, who would never let her down, never drop her. She trusted him, because he'd proven trustworthy. And he would not on his life foist off the responsibility of personal flyer onto anyone else.

I consider this again, in wonder. The little girl inside me, the child longing for relief from worry and longing for safety, but also, *also* loving a good solid adventure, takes on Peter Pan's voice, a voice

I've rarely listened to or perhaps never heard before. "Wouldn't it be fun to fly? To trust God so much that you're not worried?"

This settles over me, a sparkling confetti of truth. I want to trust that much. And deep down there's no question in my soul that God is that kind of trustworthy.

But the habit of not trusting—and isn't that what worry really is? Isn't it that we don't trust? Don't trust others, don't trust ourselves, don't trust God, don't trust politicians, don't trust the world at large or our little personal spheres?—is cemented into my psyche.

If only we could get it straight in our hearts and minds and souls once and for all: Life is full of risks. No guarantees, no label on a mattress that says, "This will last you until you draw your last breath." There will be stumbles, falls. Enormous heartbreaking disappointments. Life brings a steep learning curve. But then our internal monologue takes a wrong turn: *We can't trust what we see and we can't always trust who we see. We can't trust others to take care of us, not really. We are it, baby girl.*

Welcome to the face of worry.

But if that's all there is—if that's it, if that's the whole truth—then we are in trouble.

Worry becomes part of the gravity that weighs us down, dragging us to earth. Rather than acting as an external ballast, as the weight on the other end of the cable that pulls us skyward, worry is rather like filling our bellies full of iron shavings and wondering why we can't waddle, let alone take wing. We don't soar with worry; we create dog runs along the worry wire outside our cages.

Worry doesn't have to win. Though a prevalent part of our lives, worry can still tutor us. Before the invention of airplanes, Charles Spurgeon said the Holy Spirit is "training us for the skies."[1] Isn't it so, that all of our life is to prepare us for heaven and to invite others to come along?

When we notice worry, it teaches us where we aren't flying, where we aren't trusting. Our design, trust-wise, is a brilliant move on the part of our God, who is not limited in space or in time, to weights and gravity, air currents or groundings.

This is part of the blessing, part of the gift of our design, because? Because it forces us to make a decision about the present moment.

Just like Peter Pan had harness and pulleys and cables and ballast, multiple experts backstage to assure an excellent flight, so our fly crew and apparatus are extensive. We have everything we need to live worry-free, unbound by the gravity of mistrust.

Part of our invisible expert fly crew covers us from heaven. The Scriptures tell us that God "will command his angels concerning you to guard you in all your ways; they will lift you up in their hands, so that you will not strike your foot against a stone" (Psalm 91:11–12).

Who knew that angels had hands?

Notice with me: God says we are guarded in all our ways. All of them. Even when we think we are under the radar, or lost on a tiny capillary of a back road or on a trickling tributary and sucked into the mud and forgotten, God still guards us. So the worries that surround us, the very real issues that confront us as we consider life and loved ones and future, even then God guides us, sending angels on these heavenly assignments.

It isn't that we need a new navigation device. We just need the heavenly viewpoint. This all fits together, and one day we will see it. Meantime, we keep coming back to the truth.

If the angels guard us in all our ways, then, remind me: Why am I worrying?

In a world where people write bestsellers about zombies, vampires, and other undead, speaking of angels is still regarded as wacky. But didn't Jesus say about children, "Their angels in heaven always see the face of my Father in heaven" (Matthew 18:10)? What comfort is ours! We have felt alone and isolated with our worries, but we have angels constantly before God's face.

Sometimes, when I tucked our kids into bed, I recited Scripture over them. One of those verses, perfect to wing them off to sleep, was Psalm 34:7: "The angel of the Lord encamps around those who fear him, and delivers them."

Psalm 103:20–21 affirms, "Praise the Lord, you his angels, you mighty ones who do his bidding, who obey his word. Praise the Lord, all his heavenly hosts, you his servants who do his will."

The angels do God's bidding! They carry out God's will.

Then we are in good hands. Or wings.

If Peter Pan couldn't trust her personal flyer, she was in trouble. The harness, the cables, the pulleys were worthless if her flyer couldn't hold her weight, couldn't guide and direct her.

The same is true for us. The child in me wants to weep at this: What if we can't trust? What if our flyer can't hold our weight? But swiftly on the wing comes the truth: We can trust our personal flyer, the Holy Spirit. The Spirit of truth is our advocate and lives in us (John 14:16–18), is the promise from Jesus that we will never be orphans, never be unprotected. Jesus tells us that the Holy Spirit speaks truth to us, reminds us of what we already know, comforts and strengthens us (see John 14:25–26). This is our powerful ally in the war against worry: Invite the Holy Spirit to tell us the truth. Ask for comfort, for conviction in the midst of our anxious thoughts.

One of the most powerful lies of the evil one is that we are alone, isolated, and this is like blood in the ocean: It creates a feeding frenzy for the worry sharks. But the Holy Spirit is given to remind us that we are not alone, not ever: We are not orphans, we are not abandoned.

People on the ground form a vital link in our fly crew. We need people grounded in Scripture and emotional maturity, a pairing that equals heavenly wisdom. People who will remind us of the truth: Life is hard, of course, but look at it from outside the storm. "You will get through this," they will tell us, "we will get you through this," and not only that, but they will remind us that God is faithful and cite instances where we have both seen that faithfulness. They will tell us that the angels are doing God's bidding in our lives, that we are not alone. They will speak the truth to us with love and challenge us in the thick and confusing darkness of worry.

I have some ballast friends in my life, women who've stood by me for years, watched me twist my fingers into knots until they were raw and then held them in their own strong grasp. They've called me back to faith, assured me that God would provide. They've cheered me on, prayed me forward. They've helped me fly.

This morning, my Scripture reading included James 4:10: "Humble yourselves before the Lord, and he will lift you up." Lift you up? Lift me up? I sit with that. Even though once I'd memorized the entire book of James, I'd entirely forgotten about this principle.

Is it possible that an element of pride comes with worry, fear bloating our souls like Sumo wrestlers, but also a certain implication, "I am ultimately in control"?

If worry is remotely related to pride, then humility becomes a means of learning to let God—or trust God—to fly us. James tells us to submit to God, resist the devil, come near to God, wash our hands, purify our hearts. To grieve, mourn, and wail.

It sounds like a dreadful journey to being airborne.

And yet, we try to seize all of our tomorrows in our tiny frightened impotent grip, and end up incapacitated by our worries. Worry clips our wings.

So the opposite of this, of taking it all on ourselves, is humility. To humble ourselves.

Every time we catch ourselves on our worry treadmill, what if we simply bowed down? Maybe literally—every single time I catch myself wrangling and writhing, I literally get down on my knees, confess my pride, my attempts to manage the future, the present, the past.

And then what? I'm emptied of all that keeps me from flying.

Big breath. And then what? "And he will lift you up." God will. Not, God might. Not, maybe, if God is in a happy or forgiving or generous mood. Rather, if we humble ourselves in confession, God *will* lift us up.

A text from a dear friend, one of my ballast people, said she'd spent a good portion of Saturday confessing her unforgiveness, and forgiving people who'd damaged her deeply. And how, afterward, she felt light, free. Safe, she said.

Flying.

Five feet up the twenty-foot ladder my heart starts to thrash like a panicked bird in a cage. Redwood trees tower over our heads, steeples pointing toward heaven and glory. I can't afford to notice them, although better to look up than down. Fear slickens my palms as I haul one foot up after the other, the ladder shaking under my shifting weight. My harness and carabiner clips jingle against me.

Who talked me into this, anyway?

When I reach the platform, a thousand feet (or so) above the ground, the land scoops away in a giant dip. They've built the platform for the start of the Redwood Canopy Tours Zip Lines on a hill. I lean against the shelter, weak, my heart now somersaulting behind my ribs.

Add almost six feet onto that with my height, and when I stand, it feels like I'm a football field away from safe. I'm sure my lips have turned white around the edges and my face the color of old fireplace ashes.

Women from the retreat cheer me from below. They are all sizes and ages—one woman is seventy-four, and she rode the zip line. They'd had a two-year-old harnessed and zipping through the trees once.

I ask the expert at the top, who seems to be about twelve years of age, as she checks my rigging to be certain it's secure, then double clips me to the pulley system that runs along the (very long) cable: "Can you just push me off?"

"Sorry. It's against the law."

Of course. That's a lawsuit waiting to happen, I guess.

She urges me to take my time, there's no hurry (in spite of thirty women waiting below me, all harnessed and ready to go). Then again, I didn't have to go, she says. No shame in backing down the ladder.

I look back down that ladder, taller than I remembered, farther away than I'd thought. Know that I couldn't go backward, either emotionally or physically. But more than that, know that I want to soar through the Redwoods, want to experience the hoped-for joy of sailing high above the earth. The child in me waits, holding her breath, waits for the adult in me to fill my lungs with trust.

Sitting on the edge of the platform, I remind myself of the truth: This is a tested apparatus, an award-winning tour, safe-safe-safe in the midst of a thrill. They say that after the first jump, the next jump is easier. And more fun. (Assuming the cable holds, of course.)

It is, I suppose, like my life. We trust God in one instance, and God is trustworthy. The rope holds, the next jump is easier.

I'm invited to trust that God is able to carry me, that the angels are part of the cadre of helpers to bear me, that the wings of trust and hope will lift me heavenward, freeing me from worry. Trust that the Holy Spirit, in all this training for the skies, will guide and strengthen and comfort me in all my predicaments. At least for this particular second.

Isn't this second all that we have? We live our lives one second at a time, and it's possible, absolutely possible, to live worry-free one second at a time.

I have all the cables and pulleys and clips in place: Nothing, absolutely nothing, can separate me from God. The Holy Spirit dwells in me. Jesus will never leave me or forsake me. I have everything I need, absolutely nothing to lose. If something goes wrong, I gain. I get heaven.

Assuming I don't live a really long time in a coma.

Knowing women wait beneath, patient, cheering, I swing my heels in the air. Smile through my terror.

My fly crew is here.

I launch myself off the platform, into the air. The cables tighten. And I fly.

Consider the Wildflowers

To live is to take risks. It is absolutely central. Courage and risk are essential to aliveness. And aliveness is the thing that we all strive for and long for, yet sometimes barricade ourselves against out of fear . . . even as we are still longing for it. If we are not taking risks, it is for the same reason that people do take risks, namely, we want to be alive. We all want the same thing. I'm reminded of an elderly man who lives in a house with a steep wheelchair ramp leading down to the street. There is always a lot of traffic on his street and every morning my friend sees him going full speed down the ramp in his wheelchair. One day she asked him, "Isn't this dangerous?" And he said with sparks in his eyes, laughing, *"Yesss, it is!"*[2]

—Brother David Steindl-Rast

He will cover you with his feathers,
And under his wings you will find refuge;
His faithfulness will be your shield and rampart. . . .
He will command his angels concerning you
To guard you in all your ways;

They will lift you up in their hands,
So that you will not strike your foot against a stone. . . .
"Because [she] loves me,"
Says the Lord,
"I will rescue [her];
I will protect [her], for [she] acknowledges my name."

Psalm 91:4, 11–12, 14

Risk your life
And get more than you ever dreamed of.
Play it safe and end up holding the bag.

Luke 19:26 THE MESSAGE

1. One of the lies of the enemy is that we're alone, and that we deserve to be alone. When does this feed into your worry? What other lies are you listening to that you're worried like this?

2. In what ways do you try to keep yourself safe? How does that hurt you or hinder your growth spiritually, relationally, mentally? When do you tie in worry with pride? As in, "The only way I'm safe is if I only depend on myself"? How might that be pride?

3. Who is your fly crew? How often do they function as ballast for you, enabling you to risk your life and fly? When do you choose to call on them for help, and when do you try to avoid contact?

4. Where are some of the places where you've flown, just vaulted out in the air on a huge jump of faith? What part did your fly crew play in that leap? And how has that impacted your relationship with God? Your worry?

Votum

Dear God,
It's hard to mount up

166

With wings like eagles
When I'm afraid of risk
Afraid of heights
Afraid of falling
Afraid you aren't trustworthy.
But I'm weary of this timid
Life
And tired of allowing
Worry to win
To drag me down
And keep me down.
I want to fly.
Yes.
I want to fly.
Heal my clipped wings
Help me to trust
You
To assemble a fly crew
To watch
For a zip line
Of faith
In the forest of redwood trees
That is my life.

Benedictus

Dear Child!
You're never without
Your personal flyer
For I have said—and
I mean it!—that
I will never leave you
Or forsake you.
So climb the ladder
Secure the harness
I will not allow your foot
To stumble

Come!
We will ride on the wings
Of the dawn
And your joy
Will be made full
And your heart will sing
And we will laugh.
How we will laugh.
So come along.
Climb the ladder.
Let's fly.

12

Can I Really?

The Tool of Progress

Canning peaches and the miracles of perfection. Not.
But no worries, there's another batch on the stove.

Would anyone be interested in meeting in my kitchen to learn how to can peaches?" my friend's newsletter invited.

She's as warm and welcoming as the sun in March and lives her life open to others, sharing learning experiences with uproarious laughter and a heavy hand with the seasonings of grace and wisdom.

I imagined her kitchen: warm, bright, filled with beautiful pieces of art, an aged china cabinet few others in the universe would consider suitable for a kitchen but which creates a dramatic focal point and companion in the space. Her entire home is like a visit to a country store and an art museum, and she, one of the few people who can pull off this aesthetic combination in a way that leads guests toward God.

Without considering my calendar (still a ridiculous hash of commitments and unmanageable deadlines and also some dreadful and painful work), I emailed back. "I would love to learn to can peaches!"

Surprisingly (or not), I was the only person who responded.

And so I found myself standing in her country museum, an apron lashed about my waist, with pots of water trying to boil on the stove and succeeding only after the temperature in the kitchen had reached about 150 degrees. On the floor beside us, a basket of peaches waited, not divulging any secrets about the difficulty of our upcoming task. The rest lolled on a tarp in the garage. My friend had found a source selling baskets of mostly overripe fruit at a steep discount.

Her home is a treasury of memory, yesterday preserved for today, stored up and restored to provide grace as needed. And so has my friend been preserved and restored, squeezing the sweetest nectar from the overripe fruit of suffering and trials, missteps and miseries en route. Her life is a fragrant aroma, a gem of mindfulness, a place where worry rules nothing and instead, worship reigns. She has preserved God's presence in the Ball jars of memory, God's provisions yesterday forming her faith meal today. When needed, she pries open the contents to the accompanying pop of a broken seal, air rushing into the jar, and yesterday's fruit pouring out.

She has learned the art of learning.

Learning, of course, is an operative word for just about any new endeavor. How do you know, if you've never done something before? How can you entirely second guess every possibility, weigh all potential problems, and end up with a perfect score? Life isn't like that, and ultimately, we learn best by doing, finding out what did or didn't work, and then trying again.

But in this faith enterprise—well, honestly, in canning peaches, too—I expect to try and never fail. I want to get things right the first time, and if I don't, I will then chastise myself forever, and follow up with worry and dread and stewing about the next time. I expect to get things right—not have to apologize repeatedly for all my personal failures—and fly through the air with the greatest of ease.

Without any flying lessons, or canning lessons, in this instance.

What I fail to consider is that life and new adventures, people, work, and problems bring their own learning curve. The saying goes, "If at first you don't succeed, try, try again." What the perky sis-boom-bah cheer doesn't say, and should, is, "*When* at first you don't succeed, try, try again." And also, if you succeed at first, we'll call it beginner's luck because next time you'll be a colossal belly flop.

I didn't graduate from the School of Positive Thinking. I'm not sure people who worry can enroll.

One find for our peach-preserving day was a bushel of cling peaches. I've never thought or cared about the difference between freestone and cling peaches. The peaches taught us quickly.

Guess why they're called cling peaches?

We found out, as we cut and scraped the fruit away from the stone inside. That fruit clung to the peach stone like a starving orphan to a rock, hoping it will turn to bread. Regardless of how ripe the peach, we learned no secret of quick release to separate stone from fruit.

Near my hometown in southern Indiana, a peach orchard reaches many arms toward heaven. Both my grandfather and my father often stopped there en route from work, bringing home a small cardboard basket with a wooden handle. Round, sun-soaked fruit filled the basket, so sweet I wondered why the honeybees weren't flying in formation. The mysterious peach fuzz covered the thin skin, and the first bite tasted of heaven. Maybe Eve actually bit into a peach instead of an apple, because the pure rush and melting texture should probably be forbidden and likely holds some key to eternity.

But peaches don't last forever, and though we can hold them in a dark place in a brown paper bag to ripen, there's a point when it's too late. This, like just about everything else, I learned the hard way, when I found the last basket of peaches my grandfather ever gave me, carefully wrapped and in my pantry. Thoroughly rotten. I've never forgotten the bitter taste of disappointment and loss of allowing that treasure to disintegrate. Like I'd betrayed my grandfather's trust and generosity, and his faith in me. I, the grandchild of two farmers. I still see his face, like a well-worn leather jacket, a rare smile beaming as he handed me that basket.

This is the effect of worry plus perfectionism: I should have known better. And I shouldn't have wasted that precious gift. And I shouldn't . . . on and on trails the should and shouldn't list, and it steals the fruit that is today, that is this particular moment. All the forgotten peaches of my past worry me with their failures and that shame bleeds into my today, poisoning it as if I'd canned a little botulism last year and served it for today's breakfast.

But worry does more than leech disease into today. It reaches its tentacles into tomorrow, so that yesterday contaminates today and then runs, rancid, over those fragile moments yet unborn.

The worry stone, stuck to the fruit of the peach of today, of tomorrow.

"My hands are all cut up from peaches yesterday. But what a fun day we had!" I noted in my journal. "Such a satisfying day."

I keep seeing the luscious orbs of sunrise as we peeled their flannelly coverings and the inside took my breath away. All that glory, hidden under the skin. And only God, and now we, knew about it.

And inside—some of the peaches so ripe the stone or pit splits apart, and inside the pit is a tiny almond-shaped seed. But it's hidden. My friend had no idea it languished like Rapunzel in the prison room, waiting for someone to set her free from the armor of the knobby outer guard.

Ah, but the fruit—so sweet and slippery with its fresh juice, sometimes the slices ended up on the counter or the floor or in our mouths. They dissolved, melting over our taste buds. For lunch we savored the fruit too ripe to freeze or can, a bowlful of the sweetest candy on earth.

We ate on the patio, made from bricks my friend picked from the city garbage, with the fountain burbling in the background that she'd spent three summers getting to work.

Process. Life is a process, and there is time. There will always be time, and when there isn't, we will be in a place where time ceases to matter, for forever. Perhaps this is the secret to releasing the peach of tomorrow from the stony pit of worry: process.

That day was so stifling hot; as I remember it, the sweat ran down my face. But the laughter—my friend's "we can't mess this up because it's all fun, it's all bonus" attitude taught me that it's okay to have a learning experience. You don't always—okay, rarely? never?—start out with a mastery level of skill.

Living is a lifelong mastering process, a lifelong learning curve. Someday, I hope to live in that grace. Like, the other day, when one of my kids phoned. Life kept falling apart, absolutely disintegrating, it seemed. "I'm on such a losing streak."

A split second of pulsing painful silence. And then the words showed up for me: "No, not a losing streak. A learning streak."

There it is. The Tool of Process. Of Progress. Which is it? Both.

I'd like to really live into this truth, to speak from the experience of hard-won living, considering each day an experiment in growth and development. A learning streak. But I was born six weeks premature, not quite baked to perfection, and have been racing to catch up to myself and the growth charts ever since. In a family picture of my parents, my bouncing big brother with his enormous happy smile, and myself on my mother's lap, I look like an ancient wizened walnut with huge eyes. All of us perched as though sitting on sharp pebbles on that 1850s horsehair sofa. My mom's dark eyes look tired but so valiant, as if hope is just around the corner. I was six weeks old, so that was the day I should've been born, but I'd already accumulated some miles by then, as had my parents, given my still developing lungs that didn't know when to rest.

I didn't come out fully cooked and I won't die fully cooked. But if I can master the truth that this is a process, that movement is progress, then I move forward, daily.

Once I read that many depressives are also perfectionists, and I wonder, now, about a correlation between worry and perfectionism. Perfectionists don't allow grace for learning, as if we need to have everything already figured out. There's no room for mistakes; those take valuable time and we're already behind. And don't worriers live this way, too? Part of our worry is that there is time and space for only one right way and we're pretty sure we can't make that happen. It's like driving with both the brake and accelerator pressed down. Slow going.

Progress means to move forward, which in turn means we must move away from wherever we've been standing—from wherever we've been spinning our wheels in worry ruts. If we aren't progressing in some way, we likely aren't growing. And if worry doesn't stunt your growth, it sure doesn't put hair on your chest of faith.

All those years of worry, I've missed so much opportunity. If worry keeps me from risking, keeps me from moving forward, then

I've lost a lifetime of opportunity to grow, to love, to change. To find Christ's presence in new ways. To reveal Christ's presence in new ways. To see the worries as opportunities not just to trust, but to grow up in some way.

I'd probably be a much deeper, or kinder, person if I hadn't been clamped in worry's gargoyle claws, if I hadn't been possessed by the worry that I couldn't fix the unfixable and therefore was a failure.

But I convinced myself that worry not only showed that I cared, but that I wasn't a failure. Maybe worry even gave me a mental edge of superiority over non-worriers. Because I *am* sensitive. I am somewhat aware of the needs of others and all the potentials for disaster. I am informed. I am more alert.

Worry as a virtue? I should go into politics.

The day after our peach-canning experience, I woke up thinking that writing is like canning is like life: preserving the present for future enjoyment, storing up today to use for tomorrow.

Writers rely daily on canned goods: our memories, for instance, as we rummage through our pantries for story, image, relevance.

Writers gather the words, sort them on the tarp of paper or screen, run them through the hot bath of thought and analysis, of comparison and contrast. We peel and pare them, examine them, stuff them into containers, filled and sealed against the erosion of time. Protected from the forgetfulness that comes with passing seasons, a winter of deaths, a spring of new beginnings. And, those places of waiting for a new harvest of words to preserve for the future. Preserving. Canning. Here, we find it possible to once again break open the past for use in the present.

Isn't this process? Isn't this progress, for all of us, and we who worry? To move forward, we break open our past experiences with God, with life. With the succulent fruit of God's faithfulness spilling over our palates, we taste and see, again and again, that the Lord is good. The Lord is good, was good, will always be good.

So the fruit of our labors wasn't perfect? It still sustains. So we had a long way to go perfecting *that* batch. Shrug. We are learning. So the texture is a little mealy. Well, next time. Rather than preserving the mistakes of that crop, we preserve the graces: the color, the tang. The laughter and warmth of friends, learning together, repeating an ancient kitchen ritual known by our mothers and their mothers. A redolent time, dust motes on shelves of glistening jars, color beaming from the inside.

But like the Pink Panther, worry always peeks around the corner, skulking, stalking. After my difficulty connecting with the leader for an upcoming retreat, she emails with the not-very-surprising news that they are canceling. My mental calculator clicks keys instantly, and I realize that the next couple of months are a financial joke. We are headed into Widow of Zarephath land; prepare for three years of famine.

The fire truck could be revving its engine now in response to the clanging alarms in my head. Get this: I find myself actually thinking, "If I knew what other figures might be coming in, I would know whether I should worry or not."

Yes, Jane. Always. You should always, definitely, worry.

So I decide to practice, and go to the shelves of canned goods. What preserves can I use here? Recognize that today things are working just fine. Next month is thirty days away. God has loads of time, and here we are, years and years after leaping (or lurching) by faith out of a steady ministry and paycheck and into the churning waters of nonprofit and faith-based living. We're doing pretty well at the nonprofit part, as in, no one's making much profit around here, but I'm not doing so well at the faith-based end.

Except . . . except that we're still here. And God sweeps me off my feet with his dramatic work: Women laughing. Weeping. Healing. Learning freedom. Finding forgiveness. Reconciling. Releasing yesterday from their frozen, clutching fingers and living today. Finding God.

Instead of carrying salmonella around, I pop the lid off a jar of peaches, soft and luscious memories of God's faithfulness. Yes, those peaches. The ones we learned on. The progress peaches.

And they are sweet. Sweeter than the honeycomb.

Weeks after our peach-canning day, I told my friend that we were eating the preserved fruit I took home. She laughed her room-filling, soul-filling laugh. Then, kindly, "Jane, you don't have to eat that batch. We'll make more, and it will be better."

Possibly, worriers aren't very good at grace, at "next time it will be better" thinking, at a "try, try again" life philosophy. Though it seems like overdeveloped responsibility, if not pure vanity, that leads to the belief that we have to get it right the first time, that there's no room for learning.

I couldn't imagine all that work and fruit going to waste. But the fear that there won't be any left for later when we really need it nestles in there, too. First cousins of fear: worry, perfectionism.

My neuroses are like this winter's forty-five-car pileup on I-94. There is almost no end to the wreckage.

Not yet. (But read the next chapter.)

Anna Quindlen said, "What is really hard, and really amazing, is giving up on being perfect and beginning the work of becoming yourself."[1]

If life is designed to shape us according to the image of Jesus, then progress and process are built into the entire cooking project. Of course we're all half-baked today. Of course we have miles to go in terms of development; otherwise, we'd already be in heaven. Maybe we have wasted a lifetime by worrying. But don't we have the rest of our lifetime to go?

When Jesus says in Matthew 5:48, "Be perfect, therefore, as your heavenly father is perfect," the Greek word translated *perfect* means "mature," making progress in becoming who we're intended to be. The root word, *telos*, means "result, outcome, finish, goal."

As though life were a finishing school, and when we graduate we will have made it. Graduation meaning heaven.

Where, then, do we get the idea that we need to already have arrived at perfect? If we had, then there would be no need for Christ. "You see, at just the right time, when we were still powerless, Christ died for the ungodly. . . . But God demonstrates his own love for us in this: While we were still sinners, Christ died for us" (Romans 5:6, 8).

At just the right time. In the nick of time. The timing couldn't have been better.

After a day of good news/bad news/I-don't-think-I-can-pull-this-off news, I consider this. I want to have an eternal perspective, but also, I realize that some things are partly or entirely out of my control. And, that I don't have time until next week to worry.

Should I schedule worry, then, so that it has its place and I can gnaw and gum the issue to bits, then when I've thoroughly masticated my soul, mind, and everything around me, shift my attention to Christ? To the absolute certainty that I can't change anything, I can only give everything I have to cooperate and trust that God's strength is sufficient in my weakness?

The idea of scheduling worry appeals to me. "Sorry, I can't fit you in to my full calendar at the moment. Maybe next week?" And then next week I can be too busy, too, and can postpone the appointment. I'll get back to you on how that works.

If we can postpone worry, then it allows us space to process, to move along the continuum of reality and faith and growth. James describes the very process of becoming:

> Consider it pure joy, my brothers and sisters, whenever you face
> trials of many kinds, because you know that the testing of your

faith produces perseverance. Let perseverance finish its work so that you may be mature and complete, not lacking anything. If any of you lacks wisdom, you should ask God, who gives generously to all without finding fault, and it will be given to you.

James 1:2–5

No-fault growth options—God doesn't judge us for not knowing what to do next. But God wants to be part of the process, wants us to ask for wisdom. We aren't born mature and complete; we move in that direction, every day and every time we ask for wisdom from God and then hang around to wait for an answer.

Now, if God will speak louder than our worry, we'll be in good—or better—shape.

Scripture directs us to the process, to the production of fruit, to the addition of ingredients in the great kitchen of life:

Make every effort to add to your faith goodness; and to goodness, knowledge; and to knowledge, self-control; and to self-control, perseverance; and to perseverance, godliness; and to godliness, mutual affection; and to mutual affection, love. For if you possess these qualities in increasing measure, they will keep you from being ineffective and unproductive in your knowledge of our Lord Jesus Christ.

2 Peter 1:5–8

The main dish still needs ingredients, so we keep adding to the mix. In ever increasing measure.

Maybe most people master peaches immediately. We were still experimenting. How can you know until you learn, try, sample, and learn some more?

It's like all-day kindergarten, except it's whole-life school. Life (and canning peaches) is a project.

We have to honor the project of life, of living. Life is a process, becoming mature is a process, just like moving from infancy to adulthood. It takes a lifetime to live, and a key ingredient in that time line is kindness mixed with a dose of reality. Who do we think we are? Jesus? He was perfect so that we can be complete in him, through his work for us. It's the only way to create a life formula.

Apart from him, we are never complete. Through him, we're being made perfect. In between, a lifelong journey of learning, forgiving, growing, back tracking, trying again.

Canning peaches is like canning summer, or the sweetest moments of childhood. The firefly nights and bicycle days, the laughing sprinkler moments, all without the mosquitoes. And when I see those peaches, I don't worry: I have food for today. And for tomorrow.

And another batch, a learning batch, simmering on the stove.

Consider the Wildflowers

Come, Almighty, to deliver, let us all thy life receive.
Suddenly return and never, never more thy temples leave.
Thee we would be always blessing, serve thee as thy hosts
    above,
Pray, and praise thee without ceasing, glory in thy perfect
    love.

Finish, then, thy new creation; pure and spotless let us be.
Let us see thy great salvation perfectly restored in thee;
changed from glory into glory, till in heaven we take our
    place
till we cast our crowns before thee, lost in wonder, love,
    and praise.

—Charles Wesley, "Love Divine, All Loves Excelling," 1747

Now may the God of peace, who through the blood of the eternal covenant brought back from the dead our Lord Jesus, that great Shepherd of the sheep, equip you with everything good for doing his will, and may he work in us what is pleasing to him, through Jesus Christ, to whom be glory for ever and ever. Amen.

Hebrews 13:20–21

1. When do "should" and "shouldn't" steal the fruit from today? How do they poison tomorrow, infecting you with worry? How can your "losing streaks" become "learning streaks"?

2. What levels of perfectionism do you see in yourself? How does this contribute to worry? Is there a tie-in to depression in your situation? Who has expected perfect from you, and how has this impacted you?

3. What opportunities have you missed due to worry rather than processing and progressing? Opportunities for personal growth, for relationship with God, others? Who helps you in your life kitchen, learning grace as you grow?

4. Looking back, where do you see the curve of learning, the arc of progress and process? Peaches are often canned with a stone in the jar, which preserves the bright color (and looks cool). What are some of the stones in your journey, and how can they preserve the color, the richness, of your steps?

 *Votum*

Jesus,
It's true
I want to already be
Full grown
Rather than
Full blown

With a case
Of worry.
Help me to be
Content with
Half-baked
Knowing that
The process
Is intact
And you are
The Master Chef.
In just the right time
You will provide the growth.
Season me
En route
Help me to live
Every day
The life you've given me
And the life you've
Given for me.

Benedictus

Sweet Daughter,
When I see you
I think
"You look like my Son"
more and more.
Come to me
Keep inviting me
To give you wisdom
Keep trusting me
To provide all you need
To grow and mature
To arrive
One day
Complete
In Christ

At heaven's door.
Till then
Cling to me,
Not the stones of your failings.
It's a sweet process
Break open the peaches
Tomorrow
We'll harvest more.

13

Life at the D-I-Y House
The Tool of Anticipation

Of plumbing and the sustaining antidote to worry:
"Someone is coming."

My kitchen purred with anticipation. It smelled like warm chocolate, and hope. In two hours, my best friends would arrive for a sustained writerly retreat and also to celebrate a milestone birthday. We'd planned a princess party, I decidedly unprincessy. But I love preparing meals for guests, love special touches, so I smiled, bopping about the small space.

With my husband out of town, I bagged lunches for my grown boys before they left for summer jobs via commuter trains. Long days ahead for them, and I treasured this rare brown-bag-lunch ritual in their adult lives. I always relished the idea of nurture for them in a world more likely to devour than to build.

As they readied themselves for their day, I started a gourmet birthday cake, complicated with gluten-free layers and rich, dark, sticky chocolate. I licked the beaters, the spatula, my fingers, and set the pans in the oven.

Raw chicken lay chopped on the cutting board, ready to sauté for salads. I ticked off my list: cook the chicken, wash the lettuce, set the tables. But with no counter space, the pots and pans needed top priority. I shoved the faucet to hot, handed the boys their lunches, then turned to the sink.

Wary of the kitchen space, the guys eased toward the door—trains wait for no man, blah blah blah. I started to wave them off, when the sink drain choked and gagged, then began backing up.

Backing up like someone pumped water up through the drain into the sink, like Niagara Falls had found its way into my drain-pipe. Backed up, as in, "Boys! Help me! Bring some buckets! We have to bail!"

They ran with pails, emptied them down the toilet, returned again, and again. And still water gushed upward from the pipe.

"Mom. I think you need to turn off the water underneath the sink. That's clean water coming up the drain." My sons, so cool and observant and rational.

"No, no, no. I'm sure it's fine. We're not turning off the water. We need running water today. I'm sure it's fine." The water *spurgled,* a reverse bilge pump. I looked again. "Well, maybe not fine."

They ran more bails to the bathroom out of sheer tolerance for my naïveté. Then, "Mom, really. I think—"

In two seconds the water lapped the top of the sink, a veritable Ohio River during spring thaws.

"You're right!" I shouted. "Turn off the spigot!"

They complied, then dashed for their train. I surveyed the kitchen disaster. Raw chicken contaminating knives and cutting boards. Chocolate hardening on bowls and counters. Lettuce to wash. And guests coming—I threw a glance at the clock—in an hour.

By the time they arrived, the dishes were clean, the counter spot-less, and the bathroom—well, the bathtub doubled as a kitchen sink for the time being.

For their entire visit, an overnight, with our kitchen sink out of order, after every meal they crowded into the little bathroom with me, developing a bucket brigade of sorts between kitchen, tub, counter, and towel-drying. Patient as all get-out, tolerant of the rustic conditions.

Friends.

And underneath the camaraderie, I thought, "Rich heads home in two days. He'll fix the plumbing."

For two days, that thought sustained me, kept me from discouragement over the kitchen predicament and inconvenience to my friends and family. Anyone else might have been embarrassed, but I'm not that sensible. I had run into my total powerlessness, and it felt good. Because the end of me is the beginning of another. The refrain kept singing, "Someone is coming, someone is coming."

The anticipation of my husband's homecoming, of someone coming to fix the flood, stayed my panic and irritability and erased my worry if not the inconvenience.

The gift of anticipation. Isn't this the opposite of worry? Worry imagines with dread what's ahead, predicting the worst. But anticipation allows for the possibility of goodness. Anticipation allows us to hope for the best, God's best, rather than agonize about potential awfulness.

Anticipation isn't a Pollyanna view, all of us sitting around singing Joy-Joy-Joy songs while our house burns down around us. It's a clear-eyed look at reality: Yes, life is hard. Bad things happen. The world doesn't operate on our timetable or value system. People make choices that hurt us, or themselves, which hurts us nonetheless. We make mistakes, and those trail after us as well. Anticipation requires an honest acknowledgment of life's difficulties, a true Situation Report.

But hope, while living in the reality of today's Sit Rep, still believes in God's workings leading us into tomorrow. Anticipation reminds us that God is already there, in the future, that Jesus has gone ahead of us to prepare a place for us (John 14:2), and we can step toward that with a settled heart.

This confounds our worry tendency, but knowing that's the truth doesn't make shifting gears from worry into anticipation an automatic adjustment. It's more like learning to drive with a clutch and four-on-the-floor: so much stalling, jerking, slipping backward, killing the engine over and over. Seamless shifting takes time, practice, and a whole lot of frustration and honking horns around us.

Worry is a spiritual and relational choking, spluttering, wasting of time, and we've mastered that technique and set the car on cruise control. We can unlearn the robotic default of worry. We can learn to drive a stick shift, the one that drives us into hope. I promise.

With the plumbing issue, though it's so minor, I looked at the facts, the inconvenience, and also my own impotence. Absolutely nothing changed the situation. We streamlined the process a little bit, but then I had to let go. Someone was coming who could fix it.

What a waste of a precious two days, if I'd worried about something I couldn't fix, while I had friends in the middle of my life and all of us trying to craft words to help the world live a little bit better.

But the ineffectualness of worry doesn't change the fact of worry. Anticipation, however, does.

Worry is a forward and frightened stare at what has not yet happened. (Our mind whispers, "Might happen. It *might* happen. Be prepared.") Anticipation isn't just a spin job: For people of faith, it's the truth.

Someone is coming. Isn't that our great sustaining hope? That regardless of whatever else betides us, Someone is coming. When the people raced to the Jordan River, full of excitement at John the Baptizer's presence there, he said, "Someone is coming!" (See Matthew 3:1–12.) And before long, we hear more good news, hope: "I will come back and take you to be with me," Jesus said (John

14:3), and one day, all our dark worries will dissolve in the perpetual daytime of life with Christ. Meantime, of course, there's today. What's the plan for today?

The resident rushed up to my friend. "Miss Patty, Miss Patty! I have the afternoon off!"

Patty works at a large residence center for intellectually challenged adults. The sweet lady before her was a favorite. "Wonderful! What will you do with your free time?"

A huge smile spread across the woman's face. With a breath that filled her entire body, she said, "Oh, just be happy."

What a luscious agenda to anticipate. What will you do with your free time?

Just be happy.

How delightful, to look forward to an entire afternoon of simple happy, to reserve that space to simply be happy.

I'm not sure it will sell in the marketplace, but this alternative beats worry all to pieces. Happy. Such joy as she anticipated happy. To contemplate, not all the people and problems drilling into our skulls, but rather, all the happies around us. Just think. Right there, in the living room, or front yard, or walking down the street. Happy.

Happy has possibilities, we agree. But worry sees problems racing toward us on the street, peeling around corners to get to us, to complicate our lives and the lives of people we love. Anticipation is the opposite. Anticipation is hope, and each day an opportunity. Paul tells us, "Therefore you do not lack any spiritual gift as you eagerly wait for our Lord Jesus Christ to be revealed" (1 Corinthians 1:7). We don't lack the necessary gifts to look ahead, to eagerly wait for Jesus to be revealed! In today, in tomorrow, in all the unknowns and uncertainties and flat-out question marks of our lives, eagerly waiting, like kids watching out the window for Jesus to be revealed.

A drunk driver nearly killed Karen in the line of duty. "Within moments after the impact of the accident God revealed himself to me. His miraculous intervention spared me from death in the collision," she says. God had been pursuing her for years, and in a rush she saw that God had saved her life. She should be dead, but instead was alive. If she'd been in a slightly different (and more typical) place, the car would have crushed her.

She stopped running away and ran straight into God's arms.

After the accident, she required more than a dozen surgeries to regain use of her limbs. Since her wake-up call, Karen refuses to worry and instead eagerly waits for Jesus to be revealed. She reentered the service profession, but rather than law enforcement, tends people as a manicurist. Every morning she rubs her hands together, praying, "Wonderful, God. What do you have for me today? Who are you sending to me, so that I can love them?"

When a client cancels, rather than stew about lost income or downtime, she peeks ahead, watching for the person who needs some compassion. Client after client sits in front of her, her with her tattoos and earrings and her what-color-will-it-be-today hair. At first her clients, many of them upper class, are skeptical, but her genuine love wins them over. She loves them, and they know it. They've barely relaxed in their chairs before words tumble out of their souls, or tears down their cheeks. She sees lonely, brokenhearted, frightened people transformed by her kind attention.

Problems happen. But rather than groan, moan, and worry, Karen says, with the hard-won wisdom and experience and delight of seeing God at work, "Oh, good! I get to love someone." She seeks out opportunities, visiting the children's hospital to offer funky manicures to small cancer patients. She stops at senior-living facilities to bless the residents and tend their toes. Her payment is their joy, the relief that shines in their eyes: *Someone cares.*

She could worry. She's a cancer survivor. She doesn't have much strength in one arm. Leftover pain from the accident attacks. But she invites God to turn the worry—*Will the cancer return? Can I keep up with the needs around me? What will happen if . . . ?*—into an opportunity for hope. In everything that comes her way, she eagerly anticipates that God has someone for her to bless, to love, to give back.

And hope, like happy, will keep us alive.

To live without hope is to begin the slow atrophy of dying. But how do we conjure up hope? We can't click our red heels or tennis shoes together like Dorothy and just chant about home. Although, maybe we could: "There's no place like home. There's no place like *Home.*" And home is anywhere God lives and loves.

So home is here, right here, right now: home in us, the God who has made a home within us, royalty moving into a tumble-down tenement like our body. If there's no place like home, then we can welcome God into this moment, into this ramshackle dwelling. "Inhabit this home, this worried little hut, now, God. Inhabit my thoughts so that I am not living in worry, but living in you."

There's also no place like Home, as in heaven, and that great thought propels our minds into a new perspective, into hope. Anticipation.

One of our tools toward this perspective of hope is praise. Please don't think that trite. Praise doesn't come easily to me, worry does. My brain is like a bunch of kids bouncing on an abandoned mattress, my worries jumping up and down, turning flips, defying discipline. Let alone praise.

Romans chapter five tells us, "We find ourselves standing where we always hoped we might stand—out in the wide open spaces of God's grace and glory, standing tall and shouting our praise" (v. 2 THE MESSAGE). Wide open spaces? It doesn't feel like that, does it? And yet, we do hope that we might stand there, in those wide open spaces. Standing tall. Shouting our praise.

Wide open spaces of grace. I want that, desperately, but it is foreign to my worry-riddled brain. But wait—

> There's more to come: We continue to shout our praise even when we're hemmed in with troubles, because we know how troubles can develop passionate patience in us, and how that patience in turn forges the tempered steel of virtue, keeping us alert for whatever God will do next. In alert expectancy such as this . . . we can't round up enough containers to hold everything God generously pours into our lives through the Holy Spirit!
>
> Romans 5:3–5 THE MESSAGE

Even when we're hemmed in with troubles.

One night, alone in our house, I sorted and boxed. With several major events on the calendar, I had to ship books. Cartons and cartons of books. An enormous inventory needed to leave my storage space and travel across the country in all four directions. Would they sell? Was I wasting time and inventory? Pouring money down the drain with shipping costs?

In that dark night, I turned on all the lights even as I gnawed my lip. Then, a miracle—the Holy Spirit whispered to my worry-addled mind, "Look at all this potential, Jane. Look. All these good words, spreading across the continent, getting into people's hands and lives and hearts. Making a difference. Look at what I am going to do."

God was asking me to hope, to look beyond the boxes of troubles that hemmed me in and to anticipate his work.

So I looked. I snapped a picture of the boxes, to remember. And throughout the evening, as I carted and packed and measured and weighed and labeled, I thanked God for what was yet to come. I praised God for going before me, I thanked God for all the ways he would work in people's lives. While I was at it, I dragged out other worry inventory: I thanked and praised God for our kids, and the future God surely guided them toward. For my husband. For our uncertain future, with our home on the market and not selling.

I never ran out of worry potential, but when I ran out of words, or got distracted, I sang. Not well. Not beautifully. But I sang. Great hymns of anticipation and hope, of truth and Home. "Great Is Thy Faithfulness—Morning by morning new mercies I see." I will see, I will, I will. I sang all the more: "How Great Thou Art—Shouts of acclamation." God will take us home one day, Home, Home at last!

In the midst of that praise, the floodlight of peace poured over the worries darkening my heart. Peace, such a foreign sensation for me. Praise led me toward hope, which led me toward peace. Aren't these all the opposite of worry?

The Scriptures tell us that God inhabits the praise of his people (Psalm 22:3 KJV). God lives in our praise. Imagine that. Praise brings God's reality into our midst, into our decrepit building project that is our body for now. Praise more, worry less.

Praise. A tool for hope.

There's an interesting juxtaposition hidden within hope. It requires a certainty about the object of our hope. Which is tricky, hope being about something yet unseen.

Isn't that what Hebrews 11:1 says? "Now faith is confidence in what we hope for and assurance about what we do not see." Hoped for, not seen.

But our hope is certain, because we hope in the immovable, unshakable, unchanging God of the universe, the God who is always faithful, the God who loves without limits. The God who tells us that "Hope does not disappoint" (Romans 5:5 NIV1984) when it is God in whom we trust, in whom we have fixed our hope. The God of hope. Romans 15:13 says, "May the God of hope fill you with all joy and peace as you trust in him, so that you may overflow with hope by the power of the Holy Spirit."

Hope. Overflowing hope, Niagara Falls in our souls instead of our kitchen sinks. Because Someone is coming.

In all those flooding moments of our lives, and the trickling times as well, when worries well and spill over, anticipation is our redirect. Our hope is secure, anchored in the God who holds tomorrow—holds it, owns it, commands it—and the God of hope fills us so full that we spill over with hope.

We become people who talk about the hope yet to come. We call it to mind, like the prophet Jeremiah, and therefore we have hope. God's mercies, new every single day of our lives. Hope. We become people who live not in the dread darkness of worry, but who, deliberately, with great care, like babies learning the alphabet, form the words: "I will not leave you as orphans; I will come to you. . . . Because I live, you also will live" (John 14:18–19). Someone is coming.

We will live, here in a worry-shaded world, live with the hope yet to be revealed. All is not as it seems, the Sit Rep doesn't include God's work behind the scenes, God going before us into tomorrow. Though it appears to be dark, our God turns the dark into light and the night into day. We speak out this great truth, to a world withering for lack of hope, a world nearing peak levels of desperation for so many. Someone is coming, and we become people who walk through this world with a flaming torch of hope, offering it to others.

My finger trails down the page in the concordance, skimming verse after verse about hope. Breath catches in my throat, a Holy Spirit gulp, and I swallow around the lump of hope expanding, filling me. *Oh, Israel, hope in the Lord. The Lord, the Hope of*

Israel. Those who hope in the Lord will renew their strength. Those who hope in me, God says, will not be disappointed. Our hope is in you all day long.[1]

On and on and on, the words of hope for us, for you, for me, anticipation the trump card of all our worries. *The hope of all the ends of the earth.*[2]

Those who hope in the Lord will never be put to shame.[3]

We, this great Do-It-Yourself building project, this dilapidated shed where the Most High dwells.

We hammer away at the work before us, and hold tight, doing what we can this side of heaven, because Someone is coming.

Of this we are certain, just as a woman in labor waits with certainty and hope about the child to be born. She endures, positive that the pain will give birth to a baby, a squalling infant full of possibility and hope. And we, in labor—the pain of worry, of travail, of brokenness—also endure with hope, hope of the certainty of the coming of God, hope for a new creation. Yes, that we will be made new—process, progress!—but also the new creation, a world yet to be revealed.

All creation groans, yet we wait in hope that the transforming nature of our worries changes us for the good of others. That we might through our intersections with people, with the broken-glass places in this world, hasten the reign of God on earth. We wait, anticipating that our trials are truly nothing compared to the glory waiting to be revealed through us. *Through* us.

The glory!

Oh, hasten the hope of glory. And should it require this furnace of anxiety, do not waste its heat. Let it do its work so that our time in the smelting pot removes the dross and leaves us shining as gold. Free of worry, free to become ourselves. Free!

God, shape us through your hands, even if the pressure exerted appears to be the worries of this world. Shape us, evermore, to be like Christ, to look like Christ to others as we convey the grace of your daily bearing our burdens.

Daily! Hourly.

Minute by minute by minute. Bear us up, bear our burdens, lead us into the hope of heaven. Today.

❧ Consider the Wildflowers ❧

My hope is built on nothing less
than Jesus' blood and righteousness.
I dare not trust the sweetest frame,
But wholly lean on Jesus' name.

On Christ the solid rock I stand
All other ground is sinking sand
All other ground is sinking sand.

When darkness veils his lovely face,
I rest on his unchanging grace.
In every high and stormy gale,
My anchor holds within the veil.

When he shall come with trumpet sound,
O may I then in him be found!
Dressed in his righteousness alone,
Faultless to stand before the throne!

—Edward Mote,
"My Hope Is Built," 1834

We rejoice in the hope of the glory of God.
Not only so, but we also rejoice in our sufferings,

195

because we know that suffering produces perseverance;
perseverance, character; and character, hope.
And hope does not disappoint us,
because
God has poured out his love into our hearts
by the Holy Spirit,
whom he has given us.

Romans 5:2–5 NIV1984

1. How does hope conflict with worry? When have you battled it out and found that hope wins? Or that worry wins? What made the difference?

2. When have you anticipated something wondrous, only to be severely disappointed? How old were you when you first realized that hope doesn't always come to fruition? How has that hindered your ability to hope now?

3. The New International Version concordance lists 180 verses using the word *hope* (not counting other forms of the word). Check out Biblegateway.com and make a list of the hope verses that speak to you. Write them on 3 x 5 cards or print them out on the computer (writing engages memory muscle and helps you remember better, in case that helps). Read through a set of cards daily, even hourly if need be, to fix your mind on the hope that is before you.

4. Consider ways you can eagerly anticipate God's coming into your right-now moments. Your worrying places. What about praise: What's good, or hard, or hopeful, about praise as a practice? How about setting aside time for happy?

Votum

Lord Jesus,
I stare out the broken
Windows of my soul
The tattered curtains of my

Fixer-upper house
Flapping in the wind
I'm such a total money pit
You must be tired
Of all my broken parts
And the worry wheel
That keeps spinning
I'm so surprised
That you've moved in
But that's fresh wind
That's hope
And you love to fix
Broken hearts
So I will hammer and hold
With you
Because you promised.
And when I awaken
Every morning
A little more repair work
Finished
A few more nails in place
New curtains!
Clean windows
In this DIY that's my life
Except now it's a
Do-It-Together project
You
In me
The hope of glory
All my hope
Is in you.
P.S. The key's under the mat.

Benedictus

Dear One!
Throw out the welcome mat

Someone is coming
Soon and very soon
Meanwhile
You have a lifetime
Ahead of you
To find me faithful
To watch for me at the windows
Know this: I'm pleased
To live in you
To prepare a place for you
To walk with you through today
Into tomorrow
And one day you'll see
We're living in the midst
Of eternity
You
And Me.
Who can we bring along
On the journey
Of a lifetime?
Because hope
Does not
Will not
Cannot
Disappoint.

Worry Less So You Can Live More is, perhaps, one of my deepest heart cries. Years of plaguing worry plagued more than just me—it infested my home and attention span and compromised my family. I am honored to share this tool with you, dear reader, and pray that God will direct your heart toward heaven, and toward hope. That you will truly Worry Less and Live More every second of every minute of every day.

Please find me on Facebook or visit me at my website. I would love to hear about your journey and how God throws leis of wild-flowers about your neck and how you begin to trust more and live more and worry less and less.

And in the meantime, keep picking flowers and gathering petals. Remember, each one says, "He loves me. He loves me. He loves me."

With gratitude and joy,
Jane Rubietta

> *"All the best to you*
> *From the God who is,*
> *The God who was,*
> *And the God*
> *About to arrive."*
>
> *Revelation 1:4*
> THE MESSAGE

Notes

Introduction

1. Portions of this Introduction and chapter 1 first appeared in Jane Rubietta, "Worry, Work, Finding Delight—and knowing when to play hooky," *Conversations: A Forum for Authentic Transformation* 11.2 (Fall/Winter 2012): 38–43.

Chapter 1: Wearing Wildflowers

1. Augustine, Sermon 126.3, quoted in *Ancient Christian Devotional: A Year of Weekly Readings, Lectionary Cycle C* (Downers Grove, IL: InterVarsity, 2009), 189.

Chapter 2: Wearing Red Shoes: Trading Worry for Whimsy

1. Quoted in *Ancient Christian Devotional: A Year of Weekly Readings, Lectionary Cycle C* (Downers Grove, IL: InterVarsity, 2009), 187.

Chapter 3: The Forget-Me-Not God

1. Frederick Buechner, *Secrets in the Dark: A Life in Sermons* (New York: HarperCollins, 2006), 64.

Chapter 4: Boxed In . . . But Climbing Out

1. Saint Teresa of Avila, *Love Poems from God,* trans. Daniel Ladinsky (New York: Penguin, 2002), 276.

Chapter 5: Bread of the Presence

1. Dr. William Smith, "Definition for *Shewbread*," *Smith's Bible Dictionary,* 1901, www.bible-history.com/smiths/S/Shew-bread.

2. Goodreads, www.goodreads.com/quotes/tag/bread.

Chapter 6: Wildflower Salsa

1. This section first appeared as "A Dancing Faith" in *indeed* (July/August 2013): 7–8, © Jane Rubietta 2012.
2. Quoted in Ken Gire, *The Divine Embrace* (Carol Stream, IL: Tyndale, 2003), 11.

Chapter 7: Watered by Tears

1. This is an extreme and less common example of conversion disorder. It also manifests itself in milder forms such as numbness. It is often triggered by a sudden stress and is a form of dissociative disorder. For more information see www.ncbi .nlm.nih.gov/pubmedhealth/PMH0001950.
2. Anton Skorucak, "The Science of Tears," Science IQ.com, www.scienceiq .com/Facts/ScienceOfTears.cfm; "Tears," Wikipedia, http://en.wikipedia.org/wiki/ Tears; Sheryl Wagner, MD, "Tears—A Natural Stress Release," March 20, 2011, http://drsherylwagner.blogspot.com/2011/03/tears-natural-stress-release.html.
3. Psalm 30:5
4. Frederick Buechner, *Listening to Your Life* (New York: HarperCollins, 1992), 236–237.

Chapter 8: The Silent Walk

1. *Webster's New Collegiate Dictionary* (Springfield, MA: G. & C. Merriam Company, 1977), 373.
2. David Sack, MD, "What Makes Addicts Stop Caring? How Empathy Gets Hijacked by Addiction," SelfGrowth.com, www.selfgrowth.com/articles/ what-makes-addicts-stop-caring-how-empathy-gets-hijacked-by-addiction.
3. *Serving Life,* produced by Lightworks Pictures in association with KPI. Executive producers include Nick Stuart and Molly Fowler. The Oprah Winfrey Network film is produced and directed by Lisa R. Cohen.
4. Helen Riess, MD, "Empathy in Medicine—A Neurobiological Perspective," October 13, 2010, *Journal of the American Medical Association,* http://jama.jama network.com/article.aspx?articeid=186692, as cited by Thomas Dahlborg, "How a lack of empathy affects our healthcare," *Hospital Impact,* Feb. 8, 2011, www.hospital impact.org/index.php/2011/02/08/what_a_lack_of_empathy_does_to_our_health.

Chapter 9: Dance of the Fireflies

1. A portion of this section first appeared in "Twirling in Church," in *indeed* (July/August 2012): 7–8.

Chapter 10: School Pictures

1. Don J. Snyder, *Of Time and Memory* (New York: Alfred A. Knopf, 1999), 5.
2. Philippians 1:11; Romans 15:13; Ephesians 3:19; 1 Peter 1:8; Psalm 126:2; Matthew 9:8; Romans 15:14, to name a few "filled" verses.
3. If you are one of the millions of people who have been arrested or served time, please hear this: Your time has been served, whether you are still in prison

or imprisoned by the memories and shame. Your penalty has been paid. May the past no longer chain you, may you live free because truly, truly, "There is therefore now no condemnation for those who are in Christ Jesus" (Romans 8:1).

4. Quoted on www.Inwardoutward.org, September 6, 2012.

Chapter 11: Fly Crew

1. Charles Spurgeon, *Morning and Evening* (Peabody, MA: Hendrickson Publishers, 1995), 95.

2. Brother David Steindl-Rast, quoted in Joan Evelyn Ames, *Mastery: Interviews with Thirty Remarkable People* (Portland, OR: Rudra Press, 1997). As found at www.inwardoutward.org, January 23, 2014.

Chapter 12: Can I Really?

1. Anna Quindlen, *Being Perfect* (New York: Random House, 2005), 15.

Chapter 13: Life at the D-I-Y House

1. See Psalm 130:7; Jeremiah 17:13; Isaiah 40:31; 49:23; Psalm 25:5.
2. Psalm 65:5
3. See Psalm 25:3; Romans 5:5.

Jane Rubietta is the critically acclaimed author of fifteen books, including the award-winning *Grace Points* and *Quiet Places*. She travels internationally, speaking hundreds of times a year at women's events, churches, and parenting groups. Jane brings a voice of vulnerability and honesty as she writes and speaks on issues close to—indeed, about—people's hearts. "You've been reading my journal," women tell her after she speaks. "You've been living my life," when they read her books. About her surprising humor, they say she is flat-out funny. And no one is more surprised than Jane (except her family) when people say, "If you ever need a different job, you could go into stand-up comedy." She also writes regularly for *indeed, MOMSense, Fullfill, Significant Living,* and other magazines and websites.

After obtaining a BS in business from Indiana University, Jane completed postgraduate studies in Germany while also forming and directing an international drama team that took the Gospel throughout Europe. She attended seminary at Trinity Divinity School in Deerfield, Illinois. She is assistant coordinator and faculty member of Write-To-Publish Writer's Conference. Jane and her husband, Rich, live near Chicago, Illinois.

Jane would be delighted to discuss keynoting a conference, leading a retreat, or speaking at your church. And, as you use *Worry Less So You Can Live More* in your small groups, contact her about setting up a Skype date to meet together! To learn more about Jane's speaking ministry, itinerary, and contact information, and for a free downloadable discussion guide to *Worry Less So You Can Live More*, go to her website, www.JaneRubietta.com.